With

SAM CHOY

With
SAM CHOY
Cooking from the Heart

By Sam Choy and Evelyn Cook
with contributions by Arnold Hiura

MUTUAL PUBLISHING

Copyright ©1995
by Mutual Publishing

Library of Congress Catalog Card
Number: 95-78398

First Printing October 1995
1 2 3 4 5 6 7 8 9

Casebound
ISBN 1-56647-098-6

Softcover
ISBN 1-56647-109-5

Mutual Publishing
1127 11th Avenue, Mezz. B
Honolulu, Hawaii 96816
Telephone (808) 732-1709
Fax (808) 734-4094

Printed in Taiwan

With
SAM CHOY
Cooking from the Heart

Design
MICHAEL HORTON DESIGN

Photography
DOUGLAS PEEBLES PHOTOGRAPHY

Food Stylist
FAITH OGAWA

Dedication

To my Mom and Dad—

Aloha and mahalo for all their support throughout the years and

the knowledge they have given to all our family,

and

to my wife, Carol, and our two sons, Sam Jr. and Chris, for enduring

my vigorous pace and time spent away from them.

Mahalo to:

Bert & Sharon Toyama, Russell Onodera, Maria Brick, Amy Tanaka, Jon Kunitake, Kenny Llanes, Carol Carroll, Island Pottery, Julie Warner, Rocky Asing, Gary Wagner, Jon Pacini, Mark Santiago, Shirley Yamamoto, Ken & Roen Hufford, Babs Miyano, Amy Ogawa, Brian Souza, Greg Osowiecki, Sr., Lloyd Kaneshiro, Ted Kaaekauhiwi, Adaptation, Thomas Kaohimaunu, Brian Lievens, Mel Arelano, Aulike Matsuoka and family, Janice Furuto, Tina Kendrick, Leimomi Keliikuli, Tropic Sticks, Mauna Kea, Hawaiian Connections, Snow White Linen, Kahua Ranch Ltd., Sun Bear Produce, Mother Goose Farm, Mauna Lani Bay Hotel & Bungalows, Mark McGuffie, The Myna Bird Tree, Royal Hawaiian Sea Farm, Hilo Farmers Market, Suisan Fishmarket, Hawaii Exotic Flowers, The Eclectic Craftsman, Spirit Lifter, Loui the Fish, Kevin Parks, Aka Gardner, Lee Rogers, Sue Boyz, Joe Mathieu, Mike Leitch, Deon Kane, Gallery of Great Things (Kamuela) , Brad Hirata, Sharon Merenda, Joann Ewaliko, Paul Muranaka, Tom Stoner, Staff of Sam Choy's Restaurant in Kona, Randy (Nani) Solomon, Claire Wai Sun Choy, Mauna Kea Beach Hotel, William Mielcke, Sam Choy Family, Alan Kaaekuahiwi, Terry Davis, Kirk Black, & Denise Trunk.

Table of Contents

Lowfat Recipes

Recipes marked with this symbol • are low fat.

Vignettes

Preface

by Sam Choy

In this hurry-up world of ours it sometimes seems as if there just isn't enough time to do all the things we have to do, let alone the things we'd like to. Cooking healthy, delicious, interesting meals is becoming more and more of a lost art as we increasingly choose the mass-produced fast food that seems to best fit our fast-track lives.

But it doesn't have to be that way. You don't have to go to a lot of trouble or spend a lot of time in the kitchen to prepare really good-tasting food that's really good for you—food that's made from the freshest ingredients and that literally explodes with flavor.

That's the main reason I wrote this cookbook—to provide a variety of simple, quick, and mouth-watering recipes for ordinary, everyday, home cooks, and to put adventure and excitement back into cooking.

I don't want to come across as Sam Choy, famous chef, who's trying to dazzle you with sophisticated techniques and complicated procedures that you'll never be able to duplicate at home. All I'm hoping to do is inspire you to have fun in the kitchen and light up the faces of those you cook for.

You are the creator; I'm just the guy who wants to give you a few new ideas.

And remember, whenever you cook, make sure it comes from the heart.

SAM CHOY'S KONA CUISINE
Cooking from the Heart

Food has always been an integral part of my life. I was fortunate enough to grow up in a closely knit family, and there's no question that my interest in food began in those early days at home. Through our mother, Clairemoana Choy, and our father, Hung Sam Choy, our family was exposed to a wide range of food throughout our lives—especially the broad range of local-style, Hawaiian food. This tradition forms the basis of everything I do today and reflects much of what I believe in. It is the reason I often call my style of cooking "soul food."

My mom and dad both did a lot of cooking. All the holidays were very special at our house—my parents would prepare special meals not only for occasions like Thanksgiving and Christmas, but also for Halloween, Easter, and birthdays. I enjoyed hanging around the kitchen and helping my parents prepare the food.

My mother's favorite menu at Easter and at Halloween was creamed chicken, served with garlic mashed potatoes and Harvard beets. That was standard. We knew at Halloween or Easter that she'd prepare that meal. I still serve that exact meal today—creamed chicken with garlic mashed potatoes and Harvard beets. It's just one example of how I draw from my roots to achieve what I do today.

My mom is 3/4-Hawaiian, 1/4-German, and she can whip up all the local-style Hawaiian meals. Her mother had been sent to a missionary finishing school as a young girl, where she received formal training in Western etiquette, including serving people high tea and all that. She passed those influences on to my mom.

Once in a while, my mother made it a point to take the family to the Crouching Lion for dinner to expose us to Western-style dining. She wanted us to taste and experience foods besides the local-style Hawaiian and Chinese food—dishes like Cornish game hen, lobster tail, Slavonic steak, and Caesar salad. It seems funny now, but I vividly remember thinking what a big deal it was to have Cornish game hen. "Wow," I thought, "I get to eat the whole chicken!" I believe that the way our parents exposed us to all kinds of food had everything to do with educating our taste buds from a young age.

My dad, however, was the one who was really into food. My dad is of Chinese descent, born and raised here in Hawai'i. He was always in the kitchen, whipping up everything from oxtail soup, chow mein and gun lo mein noodles, to traditional Hawaiian dishes like squid luau. He just flat-out loved to cook!

My father learned his cooking from his mother, Yuk Kiew Lee. His parents originally were taro farmers in Punalulu Valley. People tell me that my grandfather, Hong Lai Choy, used to be one of the "taro kings" of Manoa. Later, they moved their taro patches to the country, to Punaluu, nine miles from Laie. Every day, grandmother prepared all of the meals for the workers on the farm. She was an excellent cook, who could prepare the entire gamut of Chinese and Hawaiian food, so my dad was naturally exposed to all of that as he was growing up.

I love to listen to my dad talk about those old days. It truly amazes me to

hear his stories. They grew all of their own vegetables—from watercress to ong choy, Chinese parsley and green onions, to different types of squash—right there on the farm. Of course they had an abundance of taro and taro leaves, which was their main crop. Although I didn't have a chance to experience this for myself, it lives on in me through my dad's stories.

For years my dad staged many luau and hukilau in Laie. He was responsible for feeding up to 800 visitors every Saturday. The luau naturally impacted our way of life as kids growing up. I used to help my father every

weekend, from elementary school through high school.

I feel very fortunate to have been brought up in those "olden days," when life in Hawai'i was so different from today. Then, it was common for neighbors to say to each other, "Eh, come over to our house for dinner." We would share very basic fare, sometimes chicken hekka, potato salad and steamed rice; at other times we might dig into a big steamed fish, perhaps help ourselves to a big pot of stew, with a bowl of poi set alongside it on the table. I don't think people share food much anymore.

I have warm memories of going to our neighbor's house and being served freshly baked coconut cake with homemade white frosting, topped with freshly shredded coconut. It was considered a simple thing back then, and you could tell it was fresh coconut because you could still see the brownish part where they had scraped the meat out from the coconut shell. That cake was unbelievable.

In the midst of this lifestyle, our house was a Grand Central Station, a real gathering place. My friends would always meet there to go diving. I wasn't a great diver, but some of my friends were. Later, we'd meet back at our house with bags of fish or tubs of lobsters, and I'd be the one to clean, cut and cook what we had caught. I could always ask my father, "Eh, Daddy, how you do this?" So I learned a lot. Cooking became second nature to me because of my experiences with my dad's catering operation and all the cooking we did at our house.

I know many people my age and older can look back on their own child-hoods and relate to these experiences, but most youngsters today can't. I saw the old ways start to fade away in the early '70s, as the general pace of life in the islands became more hectic, and both parents had to hold full-time jobs to make ends meet. I remember seeing other kids my age go home after school to find a note on the icebox: "Your dinner's in the pot, heat it up," or, "There's $5 on the table; go out and pick up something to eat." It's okay to do that now and then, but I get concerned as we become totally immersed in this kind of lifestyle—not only does it detract from the nutritional aspects of food, but it takes some of the joy out of life.

I remember when my sister Wai Sun was a student boarding at Kamehameha School. My dad would pack all the neighborhood kids into the car every Sunday and drive from the North Shore to town to take her back to the dormitory. Driving to Honolulu, we'd pass by the beach parks at Kahana, Punaluu, Hauula and Kahana, where you could smell all the hibachis going, with the teriyaki meat, musubi, tripe stew, oxtail stew, and other wonderful things cooking over the charcoal.

That was our Sunday ritual—attend church in the morning, pile into the car, drive to town. Stopping in Chinatown, we'd walk through Oahu Market, colorful and alive with activity, the air thick with aromas. We'd eat Chinese food at Young's Chop Suey—cheap and delicious—then we'd go see a movie at the old Hawai'i Theater, and be home by 7:30 in the evening.

There may still be a few people who take the time to prepare family picnics and potlucks, but the reality is that most parents today are too busy. It's much more common to go to Costco and pick up a prepared tray of this or that, a bucket of chicken or chili from somewhere else, or simply call a catering service. We drive here, there, pick it up—boom, boom, boom—okay, we've got what we need. Gone are the days of marinating the meat or chicken the night before, soaking it in a pan or Tupperware container, firing up the charcoal, and cooking over the grill. Nobody's got the time.

I realize that things are always changing, but it saddens me because I feel that kids today are missing out on something very special, very pre-

cious. The fast-food mentality has virtually taken over our lifestyles, and the rigors of modern life have forced people to miss out on really good, home-style meals. This feeling motivates me to try my best to give people good, old-fashioned, home-cooked meals, especially local-style ones.

I believe one consequence of our fast-food lifestyle is that many young people in Hawai'i today have limited taste for food, extending, perhaps, to other matters as well. They want burgers, chicken or pizzas—and reject things that are too different or "exotic." They have no knowledge of the old ways.

Isn't this especially ironic here in the islands, where people were once used to great diversity? We grew up with many different cultures, all so vibrant, all around us. Sometimes I stop and recall the days when we would go to a bazaar or fair and find all the different ethnic groups doing their own thing—the Portuguese people making malasadas, sweetbread and bean soup; the Japanese people making sushi, shrimp or vegetable tempura, and teriyaki barbecue sticks; the Korean people doing Korean chicken or kalbi ribs; the Hawaiian people doing their Hawaiian plates. That alone was amazing, and it lights up my heart just thinking about it.

Lifelong exposure to that kind of variety is what has made people from

Hawai'i so competitive in the food business. By virtue of our cultural heritage, I believe our taste buds are naturally educated, extremely sensitized. I often say that Hawai'i people have "dirty mouths." What I mean by that is we have very sophisticated senses when it comes to taste; we really know the difference between what is good and what isn't.

I also believe that people from Hawai'i are really "advanced" as far as food is concerned. I can remember a time in the early '70s, when Hawai'i was dominated by European chefs. I learned a great deal from them, and I owe them a lot. There are many wonderful European dishes, of course, most

relying heavily on sauces. In French cooking, especially, everything has to be cooked down to nothing—puréed to a fine paste or beyond—to a point where you could almost drink everything through a straw.

Personally, I lean more towards our Asian and Hawaiian style of cooking, where I can see all of the ingredients in the food I'm preparing. If I'm using ginger, I want to see the ginger—or water chestnuts, green onions, sweet peas, Chinese parsley, shiitake mushrooms, or whatever.

Once in the '70s, when I was just starting out in the business, I remember cooking up a simple dish of chow fun for the workers at the hotel, preparing it just as my dad had taught me: cut up the ham and char siu, slice all of the vegetables—carrots, julienne celery, some onions, bean sprouts, and chives—cook it with sesame seed oil. Well, everybody loved it, except the European chefs. They said, "I would *never* eat that—the vegetables are raw." Today, even their philosophy has changed. Now, they cook everything al dente, half cooked. In that, I sense how those of us who grew up in Hawai'i were ahead of the times.

I'm very happy to see that the food movement in Hawai'i is now getting the broader recognition it deserves. We have a wide spectrum of extremely talented people who are making their mark in the high-end restaurant business, expanding the popularity of Euro-Asian and Pacific Rim cuisine. From that perspective, it's a very exciting time for food in Hawai'i, and its future looks bright.

Personally, I try not to rely too heavily on strictly European and Asian influences. I realize that we all have to be flexible, but I sometimes worry that if we tread too narrowly along this path toward Asian, Euro-Asian and Pan-Pacific cuisine, Hawai'i might become just another version of Hong Kong, Indonesia, Korea or Japan, serving food you might find in California. Nor does giving a dish a Hawaiian name make it Hawaiian.

Rather than taking an Asian ingredient and covering it with a European sauce, or vice versa, I try to draw my inspiration from the soul food traditions of Hawai'i. For example, I don't think we should take our Hawaiian-style plate lunches for granted. Plate lunches are unique to Hawai'i and, I contend, one of the most underrated meals you could find anywhere. Even here, the trend is toward Asian, kalbi-style barbecue places, which seem to be popping up everywhere. Only a handful of small restaurants still serve Hawaiian food. I believe we really need to educate people and show them what kind of food we are capable of preparing, based upon a more Hawaiian tradition.

In our effort to put Hawai'i cuisine on the map, everyone is looking for the magic. I believe the magic lies in keeping things simple. When you start with the freshest island ingredients possible, little is left to make them better. I don't think you can. Most people would agree that fish is at its best when it's freshest, not when it's five days old and vegetables are at their best right from the field.

One of the trendiest food movements across the mainland is based on the phrase "from the garden to the table." Here again, it might be something new for others, but it's always been a way of life for us in Hawai'i. If you look at how life used to be in Hawai'i, back as a child growing up, didn't everyone have gardens? We always saw food harvested from the fields and brought straight to our tables.

Growing up in Kahuku, I watched guys like Jubilee Logan, Moke Hiram, Melvin Masuda and others harvest watermelon or corn, then sell the freshly picked produce along the side of the road on big blocks of ice. My dad would stop, we'd all pile out of the car, and he'd slice a watermelon right there on the side of the road. The watermelon may have been 20 or 30 pounds, but when you're a little kid you think the watermelon weighs a hundred pounds. I'll never forsake my roots or forget where I've come from. My local-boy style, my taste for food, all the knowledge that I have been blessed to acquire—that's me. I still cook the traditional things, like squid luau. I might do it in four or five different ways, but it's been like one big cycle for me, coming full circle.

I find myself returning to memories of my father-in-law, Felix Joyce,

who was considered the best ulua fisherman on the North Shore. I remember one evening when I first started dating my wife, he caught an 89-pound ulua right from shore and I helped him carry it back to the house. When we opened the freezer, he already had three ulua stacked on each other! I couldn't believe my eyes.

My father-in-law's favorite way of preparing the fish was by pickling it, Portuguese-style, vinha dos. After marinating the fish fillets in vinegar, garlic, pickling spice and chili pepper, he would grill 'em or fry 'em up. Ho man, you talk about delicious—so oishii! He would prepare the big white eels that the Japanese call *tohei* the same way. He'd catch those, over six feet long, right from the shoreline, as well. His pickled ulua was the best, served with fried taro and rice. Today, I do a variation of my father-in-law's vinha dos ulua, and it's a very popular item. It's one flavor that once you start eating it's hard to stop. It's that good.

In another instance, when I was working at Kuilima, my friends Jeff Campoc and Isamu Isobe put together a fishing trip for some of the staff. After work on a Friday, we all went out and set up camp. Well, as any ulua fisherman can tell you, it's a hit-or-miss proposition. Anyway, it must have been about one o'clock in the morning, and the fishermen had not had any luck. I looked at the fresh octopus, unused bait, and I asked, "We get rice?" "Yeah, we get rice." "You guys like try some squid or what?" I asked. "Yeah, sure, how you going cook 'em?" I thought of an old recipe I had learned from John Akina, one of the sons of George Akina, an old-time Laie family.

First I parboiled the squid, half-cooked, sliced it up and arranged it on a bed of chopped cabbage, like you would with sashimi. I added ginger, Chinese parsley and green onions, then poured hot peanut oil over the top—shhh—sizzle 'em up. Then I put a bit of shoyu on top. I turned my back and, boom, the rice pot was empty! Wow, they had downed the squid and rice in no time.

I got up the next morning and found everybody already in the water, diving for octopus. I asked, "Eh, what you guys doing?" They said, "Sam, you gotta make that dish again; that's a winner, man!" It makes me smile to think of that; old-time flavors—that's Hawai'i.

These are just a few examples of how I draw inspiration from our shared cultural heritage. It's important to remember where these flavors come from—our pioneering forebears, strong traditions, all rooted in the rich, multiethnic soul of Hawai'i.

My knowledge of food comes from the heart. I try to keep it pure, because people eat food to nourish their bodies. I try to keep it simple, because I sense that people crave that simplicity and familiarity of things they have grown up with. At the same time, I realize we have to prepare things that will turn people's heads and hold their attention. In that sense, I also try to be innovative in my cooking.

If I have any magic, I believe it's taking soul food, local food, and adding a twist to make it memorable. The twist is the key. Using all my knowledge of food, I'm always coming up with ideas and working out ideas with the team of people that I have.

An example of this is when we took a basic Hawaiian poke and set out to refine it. We worked at refining our phenomenally popular fried poke, going through many poke recipes until we came up with one that tasted the best. Another time we put an omelet on hot steamed rice, then poured hot beef stew on top of it, creating our ultimate stew omelet. Then we took traditional gon lo mein and chow mein noodles, served them in a flour tortilla shell, and called it Sam Choy's noodle mania.

Ahh, yes, the twist. We've stacked sheets of deep-fried won ton with layers of lettuce, blended soba and somen noodles in between, and covered the top with a spicy chicken stir fry. We call it Sam Choy's Kona Cuisine Wok Salad. That's the twist.

We've marinated shrimps in a simple sauce of fresh garlic, fresh herbs, basil, dill, cracked peppercorn, a little Hawaiian salt or sea salt, and a bit of shoyu sauce; threw the shrimps on the grill real quick, leaving them pink, half-cooked; then we folded them in a ginger pesto and served it on pasta. The twist is the ginger pesto—a blend of ginger, chinese parsley, green onions, white salad oil, white pepper, and a little garlic—like you'd find on cold ginger chicken.

One of the guiding principles I think about as I create these dishes is something the executive chef at the Waldorf Astoria in New York City told me when I was working there. "You know, Sam," he said, "one of the most important things to remember when you cook is to make your meals memorable." I've taken that advice to heart and always strive to achieve that, every day, with every dish I serve.

When people come to my restaurant, I want to give them a true taste of the islands, a real sense of the flavor of Hawai'i. I want every person, whether they're from Hawai'i or elsewhere, to remember the experience. Perhaps one day, six months, a year, or even several years from now, they might be driving somewhere when they smell something and, like a light bulb snapping on in their heads, it'll make them remember the aroma, the taste of something they had eaten at Sam Choy's.

That wonderful feeling happens to me—when I go to a tailgate party or to the beach and I smell teriyaki cooking on the hibachi, it takes me back to my childhood, when my dad used to take us to town on Sunday, driving past all the parks. In my mind, I can see the dried squid hanging on the lines; the people standing around in tight, little circles, hooking oama by Punaluu; the local boys surrounding a net for akule outside Kahana Bay. These are memories that are locked in my heart—and will forever inspire me whenever I cook.

If someone were to ask, "What's Sam Choy's magic?" To me the ultimate compliment would be if someone responded, "You know that Sam Choy, he cooks local grinds, soul food, from the heart."

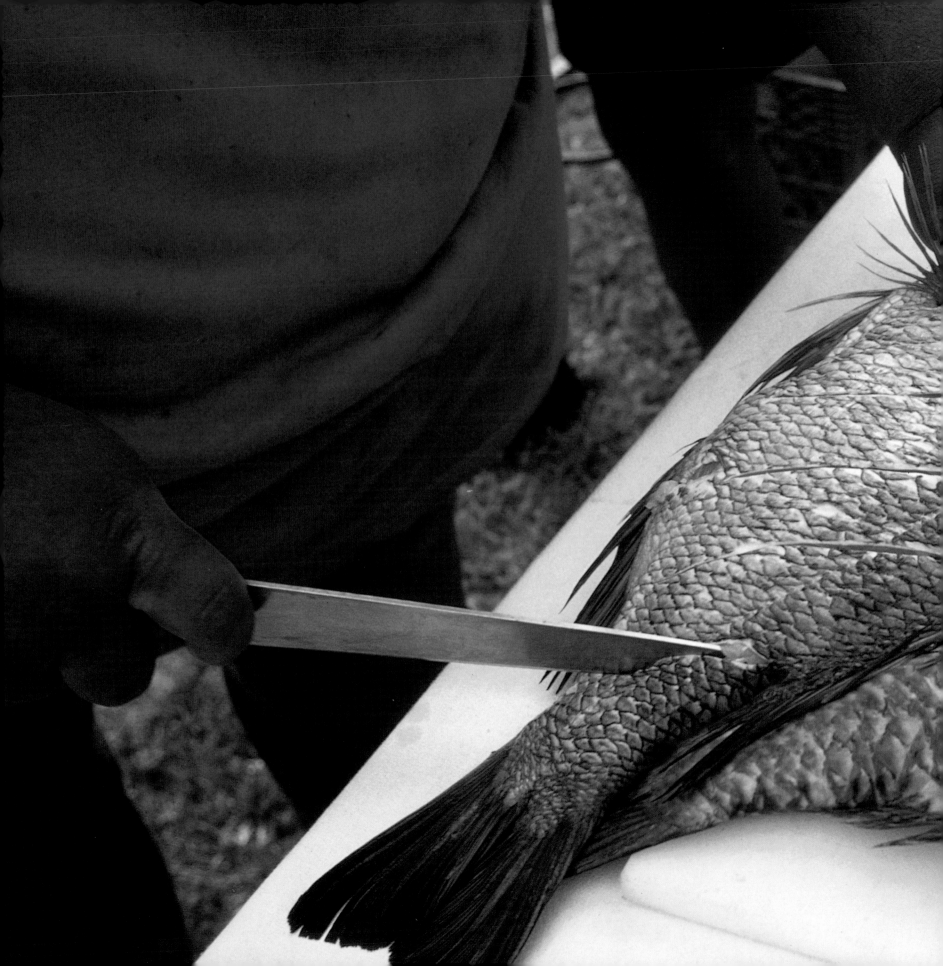

PUPU
(APPETIZERS)

Fresh-Fried Poke

Sometimes we take it for granted that here in Hawai'i we're surrounded by the ocean, allowing us access to the freshest seafood in the world. When I was a boy, my family would put on tabis and goggles, wade out to waist-deep water around the reefs of Laie Bay, and pick limu. At other times we would catch lobster for dinner, or I would go diving for octopus with my friends.

Those kinds of fresh ingredients were part of the traditional Hawaiian diet. Although today's food is high in fat and sodium, I believe that the work being done by people like Dr. Terry Shintani with the Waianae Diet is an important force in educating people to eat healthier. At least we can still learn to appreciate some of the traditional Hawaiian foods like steamed fish, limu, or fresh poke.

I sponsor an annual poke contest that has become very popular. One of the main reasons I do it is to educate people. I've always said, "Look, raw dishes like sushi and sashimi have made it big-time, with international fol-lowings. Other popular dishes are actually half-cooked sashimi, so why shouldn't poke become accepted on an equal scale?"

One day, when we were all just sitting around sharing new ideas, I said, "Let's make some poke and sear it real quick on the tempan-yaki grill." We tried many different kinds of poke before we found the best-tasting one.

It's funny now to look back at when we first introduced the fried poke at our restaurant. The first thing people said was, "Eh, don't buy the fried poke—that's Sam Choy trying to sell his old poke." When you think about it, it's almost natural that local people might think that.

I said, "Aw, come on you guys. Give me a break. What more do I have to do to prove myself to you?" Then we decided to offer samples of the fried poke in little cups. The next day, the fried poke was the hottest thing on our menu. It just took off. Today, we serve an average of about a thousand pounds of fried poke a week. It's just phenomenal.

GINGER MARINATED SEARED SASHIMI

SERVES 4 TO 6

TAKE 2 pounds fresh yellowfin tuna and cut into 2-inch by 2-inch blocks, any length. Marinate for 45 minutes to an hour in a mixture of 2 teaspoons fresh minced ginger, 1/2 cup shoyu, 1 tablespoon brown sugar, 1/2 teaspoon sesame oil, and 2 finely minced Hawaiian hot chili peppers.

After marinating, place fish on a hot hibachi or barbecue grill, searing very quickly (about 10 seconds, or less) on all sides. Slice as thick or as thin as you like and arrange on an appetizer plate over a bed of shredded cabbage (won bok, head cabbage, purple cabbage, or your favorite sprouts). Garnish with black sesame seeds and serve with the following dipping sauce:

In a blender, combine 1/4 cup minced ginger, 1/2 cup chopped Chinese parsley, 1/4 cup minced scallions or green onions, 2 cloves minced garlic, and 1/2 cup light salad oil. Blend for 30 seconds, then adjust seasoning with salt and white pepper to taste. (Do not substitute with black pepper.) Pour into serving bowls or small individual dip containers and serve with sashimi.

I look at food as something sacred, almost like religion, because of how important it is in nourishing the body and because, when it's prepared and presented in the right way, it can really bring joy. When I cook, it comes from my heart. I don't want my cooking to just fill people's bellies, I want it to make them sparkle. I get great pleasure out of capturing the best natural flavors of the fresh ingredients I use, and making people happy by presenting food to them at its highest peak of quality and taste.

SAM CHOY'S WORLD FAMOUS FRIED MARLIN POKE

I serve 1,000 pounds of this dish in my Kona restaurant each week, and I'm not kidding when I say it's world famous!

For each serving, take 4-6 ounces of raw marlin (no other fish works as well as marlin in this recipe), and cut into 3/4-inch cubes. Place cubes in a mixing bowl with 1 teaspoon shoyu, 1/4 cup chopped round onion, 1 teaspoon green onion, 1/4 cup ogo seaweed, and 1 teaspoon sesame oil. Mix well, then quickly sear in 1 tablespoon hot oil (or enough to cover bottom of pan) on high heat in a wok. Don't cook for more than a minute or two, as you want the center raw. Serve on a bed of bean sprouts, chopped cabbage, or greens.

When I cook fish I do it Chinese-style, by quickly searing it on high heat to seal in flavor and moisture; it's one of the secrets that makes the fish I serve at my restaurants taste so good. You have to be careful when using this technique, though, because if you don't remove the fish quickly from the hot pan it will overcook. Basically, you just slap the fish in the pan, sizzle it on all sides, and remove. You need to add enough oil to coat the bottom of your wok or skillet so the fish won't stick, and heat the oil until it's almost smoking before you add the fish.

MAHIMAHI MACADAMIA NUT FINGERS

SERVES 4 TO 6

CUT 2 pounds mahimahi into strips about the size of your fingers and season with salt and pepper. Bread strips, using the following basic breading method:

After seasoning fish fingers with salt and pepper, dip in flour, then in beaten eggs, then in a mixture of 1 cup chopped macadamia nuts and 1 cup panko or bread crumbs. (Start with 1 cup of flour and 2 whole eggs.)

Deep-fry breaded mahi fingers, a few at a time, for 1-1/2 to 2 minutes, or until golden brown, in oil heated 325-350 degrees. Drain on paper towels, then arrange on appetizer plate around a mound of spring mix or salad greens and serve with a pineapple/papaya marmalade dipping sauce. Add 1 tablespoon of prepared horseradish to this dipping sauce for taste (optional).

The marmalade is made by combining 1/2 cup diced papaya, 1/2 cup diced pineapple, and 3 tablespoons sugar. Simmer in a heavy saucepan for 20 minutes, stirring occasionally. Serve warm with the fish fingers.

NUTTY CRUSTED
LAMB CHOPS

Lamb is such a moist and delicate meat you want to seal in the flavor and natural juices, and a good way to do that is to encase it in a crust. It's important to keep in mind that lamb, like fish, is ruined by overcooking. Lamb shouldn't be cooked past medium. Macadamia nuts really add something nice to this recipe.

PLAN on 2 lamb chops per serving. Marinate the chops for 1 to 2 hours in a mixture of 2 cups brown sugar, 1/2 cup shoyu, 1/2 cup red chili flakes or minced Hawaiian hot chili peppers, 1 ounce finely chopped Chinese parsley, 1 teaspoon chopped garlic, and 1/2 teaspoon sesame oil.

After removing from marinade, dip chops in flour, then in beaten eggs, then in a mixture of 1 cup panko (or breadcrumbs) blended with 1 cup chopped macadamia nuts, almonds, or walnuts.

Melt enough butter mixed with cooking oil to coat the bottom of a sauté pan, then sauté chops just long enough to set crust, and finish in a 325-350 degree oven for about 5 minutes. Lamb, like fish, is something you don't want to overcook.

Serve with Kau Orange Glaze, which is made by mixing 1 cup orange juice with 1 cup sugar and 1/2 cup rice wine vinegar. Bring to a boil in a heavy saucepan and simmer uncovered for 1 hour, stirring occasionally, until it reduces down to a nice glaze. You can drop some peeled orange segments into the glaze after it's done.

Arrange the lamb chops on a bed of watercress or sprouts, with the *Kau Orange Glaze* in a side dish for dipping.

• STEAMED WEKE ULA LOCAL STYLE

START with a whole, cleaned, scaled, fresh weke ula, (1 to 2 lbs.) or fresh coho salmon, trout, flounder, or red snapper. Score the fish by cutting diagonal slices in two directions to make diamonds. Sprinkle on about 1/2 teaspoon of rock salt, Kosher salt, or ice cream salt, and place on a ti leaf (optional).

Slice fresh ginger into fine, matchstick-sized slivers and sprinkle on the fish. Place the fish in a steamer basket and lower into a large kettle over boiling water. Cover and steam for 8 to 10 minutes, or until done, but not over cooked.

Arrange on a serving platter and cover with chopped scallions or spring onions and whole sprigs of Chinese parsley.

In a small saucepan, heat 3 tablespoons light salad oil or peanut oil for about 5 minutes on medium-high until real hot (just before it starts to smoke), then carefully pour over fish. Finish by drizzling fish with one tablespoon shoyu. This dish is best when eaten with chopsticks.

If you read through this whole cookbook you'll notice I mention, more than once, how important it is not to overcook fish. The main reason people don't like fish is because they've only tasted it when it was overcooked. When fish is cooked correctly, it's delicious, especially fresh fish caught in our deep, clean Hawaiian waters. Fish is cooked as soon as it loses its translucency and turns opaque. It doesn't take long. The old-fashioned method of waiting until you can flake it with a fork is wrong. By that time, the fish is already overcooked.

DEEP-FRIED WON TON BRIE
WITH FRESH PINEAPPLE MARMALADE

TAKE a round won ton wrapper and brush with egg white. Place a cube of brie cheese in the middle. (You can add a sprinkle of chopped macadamia nuts or other nuts, if you like.) Press the cheese down while gathering up the won ton wrapper to make a little purse, and pinch the wrapper together just above the cheese to seal. The won ton wrapper should fan out a little at the top, with the overall effect being one of a miniature gift-wrapped package.

Deep-fry to a golden brown for about 2 to 3 minutes in oil heated to 350 degrees. Another option is to bake the brie in phyllo dough in a 350-degree oven for about 10 minutes, or until golden brown.

Serve with warm pineapple marmalade that you make by combining 2 cups fresh (or canned) chopped pineapple with 1 cup sugar. Bring the mixture to a boil in a heavy saucepan, then simmer uncovered for 45 minutes (less, if you're using canned pineapple), stirring occasionally, until it thickens to a syrupy consistency.

If you're in a hurry, open a jar of prepared orange or pineapple marmalade and thin with white wine over low heat for about 5 minutes, until it becomes a good consistency for dipping. If you like, add a pinch or two of hot chili flakes to spice it up.

HOT, I MEAN HOT, MINIATURE BEEF KABOBS

The usual way of making kabobs is to string up a bunch of vegetables and meat, then cook it over coals, and you can't really improve on something so simple and good. I like to make mine spicy and cook it medium rare. But remember, you are the artist and can create whatever you like. A nice touch when you have guests is to sear the kabobs right at the table on the hibachi. This recipe is a very tasty one.

FIGURING on 5 ounces per serving, take as much flank steak, or flap beef, as you need and cut into 1/2-inch cubes, then thoroughly massage into it for 2 to 10 minutes the following "dry" marinade.

To make 2 cups marinade, combine 1/2 cup shoyu, 1/2 cup salad oil, 1/2 teaspoon sesame oil, 2 tablespoons dry roasted sesame seeds, 2 tablespoons brown sugar, 1 tablespoon minced Chinese parsley, 1 tablespoon minced garlic, 1 tablespoon minced ginger, 1/4 teaspoon white pepper, and 1 teaspoon dried red pepper flakes or 2 small fresh minced hot peppers. Once you've worked the marinade into the beef, set it aside for 45 minutes to marinate.

After marinating, place on bamboo skewers, starting and ending with a mushroom cap, with chunks of beef and chunks of onion alternating in between.

Cook each side 2-1/2 minutes (for medium rare) over hot coals or on a flat-top grill and serve with *Teriyaki Glaze*.

TERIYAKI GLAZE:

1	cup *shoyu*
1/2	cup *mirin*
1/2	cup water
1/4	cup brown sugar
1 1/2	tsp. garlic, minced
1 1/2	tsp. ginger, minced
1	Tbsp. cornstarch
2	Tbsp. water

In a small saucepan combine all ingredients, except cornstarch and 2 tablespoons water, and bring to a boil. Blend cornstarch and 2 tablespoons water to make a smooth paste, then add to mixture in pan. Reduce heat and simmer, stirring frequently until thickened.

Makes 1 cup.

I enjoy going to the sources of where things are grown or raised, and one of my repeated highlights is to go up to my friend Harvey's farm where he grows some of the world's best lettuce, six to eight different varieties. It's so beautiful up there in the mountains above Honaunau, overlooking the Kona coastline way down below. I like to bring all those different types of fresh lettuces back to my kitchen and use them for salads and other dishes. One of my favorites is vegetable roll-ups, a well-known appetizer in Indonesia, Thailand, and Vietnam. The Chinese also make it, but they do it without rice-flour wrappers, using large lettuce leaves instead to roll up all the other vegetables inside.

• KONA SUNSET VEGETABLE ROLL-UPS

THIS may look like a really long recipe, but it isn't that hard and, believe me, it's worth it. For each roll-up, take a rice-flour wrapper (found on the shelf in the Oriental section of most grocery stores in packages called "spring roll skin") and soak it in water for a couple of minutes until it gets pliable. Remove it from the water and put it on a plate, then add whatever vegetables you like, or whichever ones you happen to have on hand, then roll it up.

Some of my favorites are three or four different lettuces—like lollarosa, red oak, baby romaine, and red leaf lettuce, then bean sprouts, pickled carrots, pickled daikon, fresh mint, and fresh Thai basil. These are just a few ideas to get you started, but it's really unlimited what you can do with this.

It makes a really great appetizer for a nice leisurely evening when you sit around with friends or family, surrounded by beautiful platters of colorful lettuce and vegetables and a plate of wrappers. It's fun for everybody to make their own roll-ups and dip them in an assortment of different dipping sauces you have prepared. You can give everybody their own bowl of water to soften the rice-flour wrappers. In restaurants in Vietnam there's usually only one bowl of water and everybody has to share.

The pickled vegetables you need for this dish are really easy to make. I've suggested pickled carrots and pickled turnips, but you can pickle just about any firm vegetable, such as onions, cucumbers, string beans, beets, bean sprouts, radishes, cabbage, etc.

First, you cut the vegetables into 2-inch long sticks that are about as thick as a pencil, or thinner, if you prefer. For each medium-sized carrot and turnip you'll need about 1-1/2 tablespoons of rock salt, which you sprinkle over the cut vegetables and let stand for 20 minutes. The purpose of this is to draw out the moisture and cause the vegetables to wilt. Squeeze out excess water—don't rinse.

After the salting process you need to soak the vegetables overnight in a pickling solution of 1/2 cup sugar, 1/2 cup rice wine vinegar or apple cider vinegar, and 1/2 teaspoon salt. Be sure to completely dissolve the sugar and salt.

Even if you don't get around to making the roll-ups, the pickled vegetables by themselves are great.

When you serve the roll-ups, you'll want to have several sauces to dip them in. I'll give you three different recipes here, but you don't need to limit yourself to these. Go with what you like.

SPICY CITRUS VINAIGRETTE

1/2	cup fresh orange juice
1/2	cup rice wine vinegar or apple cider vinegar
1	cup sugar
1	tsp. fresh ginger, grated
1/2	cup Chinese parsley, chopped
1/2	tsp. salt
1	fresh hot chili pepper or 1/4 tsp. dried red pepper flakes

white pepper to taste

Dissolve salt and sugar in orange juice and vinegar, add hot peppers, ginger, and white pepper and whisk for 2 minutes, then fold in chopped Chinese parsley.

Keep in mind that if you use dried pepper flakes, it takes about a half hour for the hotness to kick in, because the pepper is dehydrated. So don't add more until you've waited that amount of time to taste it.

continued on following page

TRADITIONAL SWEET AND SOUR WITH CUCUMBERS

1   cup sugar
1/2   cup vinegar
1   cup pineapple juice
1/2   tsp. salt
1-1/2 cup cucumber, sliced paper thin (one whole medium cucumber)
1   Tbsp. fresh ginger, minced
1/2   cup macadamia nuts, chopped
fresh Hawaiian hot chili peppers or dried red pepper flakes, to taste

Combine sugar, vinegar, pineapple juice, and salt, and whisk real well until everything is dissolved. Add the thinly sliced cucumber, ginger, mac nuts, and chili peppers. Give it a stir, and serve.

WASABI VINAIGRETTE

2   cups orange juice (freshly squeezed is best)
3   Tbsp. vinegar
1/2   cup oil
3   Tbsp. sugar
2   Tbsp. shoyu
1   Tbsp. salt
2   Tbsp. sesame seeds
2   Tbsp. wasabi

Mix all ingredients together and blend well. Wasabi is a Japanese horseradish that can be found in most supermarket Oriental sections. If you like hot food, you might want to add more than I've suggested here, or less, if you prefer a milder flavor. Wasabi comes in either powdered or paste form. If you buy the powder, you can make it into paste by adding a little water.

A trick I learned from the Japanese is to make the paste with warm water if you want the wasabi really hot, then turn the mixing bowl with the paste in it upside down for about 3 minutes. This causes some sort of chemical reaction that brings out the fire.

SAM'S "DA KINE" COCONUT SWEET PORK

SERVES 6 TO 8

Because of my Asian background, I like to marinate meat so that a nice flavor is embedded in it. And because of my Hawaiian roots, I like to use island fruit in my recipes. This dish represents influences from both sides of my heritage—Chinese sweet pork and Hawaiian "da kine" coconut—combining them in a beautiful blend of flavors, while at the same time keeping it simple.

This recipe doesn't take a lot of time to prepare, but you do have to marinate the pork overnight, so plan on it taking two days from start to finish. Island residents know this as "char siu" pork, but I leave out the red food coloring.

1	whole pork butt (3 to 4 lbs.), deboned, cut into strips 1 in. thick, 2 in. wide, about 5 in. long
1/4	cup rock salt
2	Tbsp. shoyu
3/4	cup garlic, minced
1	Tbsp. fresh ginger, minced
2	cups brown sugar mixed with 1/2 cup shoyu
2	Tbsp. light salad oil
1/2	cup coconut syrup
	shredded cabbage, enough to cover serving platter
	hot mustard dip

ADD the rock salt, shoyu, garlic and ginger to the strips of pork and massage into the meat for 5 to 10 minutes, then let stand, refrigerated, for 3 to 4 hours.

Pour the brown sugar/*shoyu* mixture over the pork and massage again for another 5 to 10 minutes. Let marinate overnight in the refrigerator.

The next day, in a small mixing bowl combine light salad oil with coconut syrup (the same coconut syrup as used on pancakes) and set aside.

Preheat your oven to 350 degrees. Place a roasting rack in pan and arrange the strips of marinated sweet pork on it, bake for 30 minutes at 350, then for 45 minutes to 1 hour at 250 degrees, or until the pork is done. It is very important to cook pork well, so when you think it's done, slice the thickest piece and make sure no pink juice runs out.

During the last half hour of cooking, baste the meat three times with the oil/coconut-syrup mixture, using a pastry brush.

This can be served hot, warm, or cold, sliced thick or very thin, but it is easier to slice when it has cooled.

Serve on a bed of shredded cabbage. It's great with Coleman's hot mustard dip, which is very easy to make. You take 2 tablespoons of Coleman's hot mustard powder and make it into a paste by gradually stirring in 1 tablespoon water. Then add shoyu until it reaches a nice dipping consistency.

SPICY CHICKEN WINGETTES

SERVES 4 TO 5

This is a great finger food. It's easy to prepare, and even easier to eat. Great for parties. And very addictive. You can't just eat one or two or three. I'd like to say it's "finger lickin' good," but I know I'd better not.

1/2   **cup shoyu**
1/2   **tsp. white pepper**
1   **Tbsp. garlic, minced**
1/2   **tsp. fresh ginger, minced**
1   **cup sherry**
one large bag chicken wing drummettes (about 3 pounds)
1   **cup flour**
1/2   **cup rice flour**
1/2   **cup cornstarch**
enough oil or fat for deep frying

IN a large bowl, mix together the shoyu, white pepper, garlic, ginger and sherry. Add chicken to shoyu mixture and marinate for 1 hour. Mix together flour, rice flour and cornstarch and set aside. Remove chicken from marinade and dredge in flour mixture until coated, or shake the pieces in a plastic bag containing the flour mixture.

Heat oil to 350-375 degrees. Deep-fry chicken for about 3 or 4 minutes until golden brown. After frying you don't need to drain the chicken because it goes right into the sauce.

For the sauce you'll need:
2   **cups shoyu**
1   **cup water**
1   **cup pineapple juice**
1-1/2 **cups sugar**
1   **cup scallions, minced**
1   **tsp. fresh ginger, minced**
1   **Tbsp. hot pepper flakes**
1   **Tbsp. sesame seed oil**

In a large mixing bowl add all the ingredients and whisk until all the sugar is dissolved. (You can make the sauce a day ahead of time, if you like.)

Place the hot chicken wings in the sauce for about a half minute, remove and arrange on a serving platter over a bed of sprouts or lettuce leaves. It goes great with the vegetable roll-up platter.

GINGER ONO

SERVES 6

1	pound fresh raw ono
1-1/2	cups assorted sprouts
1/2	cup *Local Pepeekeo Dip* (recipe follows)

THINLY slice raw ono. Line small platter or individual plates with sprouts of your choice. Arrange *ono* slices on sprouts. Spoon Local Pepeekeo Dip over the raw fish and serve chilled. (If you've never tried raw fish, you'll be surprised how good this tastes.)

LOCAL PEPEEKEO DIP:

1/2	cup oil
1/2	tsp. salt
1	clove garlic, minced
1/4	cup ginger, minced
1/4	cup green onions, minced
1/4	cup lightly packed Chinese parsley, minced
1/8	tsp. white pepper
1/4	tsp. red pepper flakes, or 1 fresh Hawaiian chili pepper, minced

In a small saucepan heat oil, add salt, and cook for 2 to 3 minutes. Cool. Stir in garlic, ginger, green onions, Chinese parsley, white pepper, and red pepper. Chill. Makes 3/4 cup.

Coming from a fishing village on the North Shore of Oahu, I grew up catching and eating fish as a way of life and learned early which fish were good for cooking, which for eating raw, and which for making traditional Hawaiian poke. I started playing around with preparing fish in different ways, and one of the combinations I really liked was ono sashimi with ginger sauce. People rave about how good it is. They can't believe it's ono.

SALADS

NEW WAVE MARINATED AHI SALAD

SERVES 1

This delicious salad offers an interesting contrast in tastes and textures between chilled greens, cold noodles, and warm fish. You can make it low-cal by omitting the deep-fried flour tortilla and the oil used in the marinade and using a low-fat dressing.

3   ahi fillets (2 oz. each and about 1/2 in. thick)
1   Tbsp. olive oil for searing fish (or enough to coat bottom of pan)
2-3 oz. Japanese soba noodles, or somen
1   flour tortilla
salad greens (a handful or two)
salad dressing of your choice

GARNISHES:
carrot, beet, and radish curls, or grated carrots and zucchini
3   cucumber slices
3   tomato slices
sprig or two of Chinese parsley
sprinkle of black sesame seeds, chopped macadamia nuts, or chopped walnuts

MARINADE:
(for one portion, makes about 1 cup)
1/2   cup shoyu
1/4   cup light salad oil
2   Tbsp. mirin
1/4   tsp. sesame oil
1/2   Tbsp. Chinese parsley, minced
2   Tbsp. green onions, thinly sliced
1   Tbsp. garlic, minced
1   Tbsp. ginger, minced
1/2   tsp. salt
1/4   tsp. white pepper
1-1/2 tsp. brown sugar
1/2   tsp. ground Five Star spice
1   Tbsp. black sesame seeds
1   pinch dried red pepper flakes, or 1 fresh Hawaiian chili pepper

COMBINE all marinade ingredients and blend well. Remove 2 tablespoons of marinade (or more, to taste) before marinating fish, and set aside to use later on noodles. Marinate ahi fillets in mixture for 5 minutes, or less, then remove fish and set aside.

Cook soba noodles (or somen) according to package directions, rinse well in cold water and drain. Take the 2 tablespoons of marinade you set aside and mix it with noodles. Chill noodles in fridge for 20-30 minutes.

Have everything ready to go before you cook the ahi so that the fish will be hot when you serve it. Also wait until the last minute before placing the greens and noodles on the tortilla, or it will become soggy.

When you have everything ready, sear the marinated ahi on high heat on a flat griddle or sauté pan in olive oil for about 1 minute per side. (You want the fish to remain raw in the middle.)

Place on a salad plate a flour tortilla you have deep-fried to a golden brown and arrange a handful or two of your favorite greens broken into bite-sized pieces (I like using a variety of colored lettuces) on top of the tortilla. Place the cold *soba* noodles on top of the greens, then arrange warm fish on top of that.

Put your vegetable curls or grated vegetable garnish on top of the fish, add a sprig of Chinese parsley, and sprinkle with black sesame seeds, or chopped nuts.

Place the slices of cucumber and tomato around the edge of the plate and serve with your favorite dressing. I like using my Creamy Oriental Dressing with this salad. (See *Sam's Signature Salad Dressings* at end of salad section.)

You'll notice that my salads aren't the ordinary kind using just cold ingredients. They are made special by combining Chinese stir-fry cookery with natural fresh lettuces and greens, and by the inspired blending of a variety of interesting ingredients that seem to provide a different explosion of flavor in every bite. I call them "wok salads." They are trendy and unique and have won awards, but my best reward is watching people's eyes light up with pleasure and surprise when they taste one of these creations.

FRIED MARLIN POKE WITH NORI-WRAPPED FIRECRACKER SALMON

SERVES 1

This is our famous fried marlin poke garnished with deep-fried nori-wrapped salmon. Marlin is very local, salmon is very "un-local," and the dish combines Japanese, Hawaiian, and American, or Norwegian, influences in a very interesting way. And it's really good!

Almost everybody loves this salad. The secret is to use marlin. No other fish works as well.

5	oz. marlin
1	tsp. shoyu
1/4	cup round onion, chopped
1	tsp. green onion
1/4	cup ogo seaweed
1	tsp. sesame oil
	enough salad oil to coat bottom of wok or skillet
1 or 2	handfuls of mixed salad greens

CUT the marlin into 1/2-inch cubes. Add shoyu, onion, green onions, ogo, and sesame oil. Mix well. In a wok on high heat, quickly sear marlin cubes for no more than a minute or two in hot oil, making sure not to overcook. You want the fish raw in the middle.

Serve hot on bed of salad greens with firecracker salmon and either my *Creamy Oriental Dressing* or my *Wasabi Vinaigrette*, or both.

NORI-WRAPPED FIRECRACKER SALMON:

2	pieces salmon, cut in sticks the size of your finger
1	sheet nori
	enough oil for deep-fat frying

Spread a little wasabi on the salmon sticks, more if you like things hot. Cut nori sheet in half and wrap a half sheet around each stick. Deep fry for 15 seconds.

Cultivating a True Kona Cuisine

One thing I'm very pleased about our restaurant operations in Kona is that we are able to offer our customers some of the very best food that the Big Island produces. From freshly caught seafood to locally grown produce, I am proud to serve products unique to Kona. Poi from Waipio Valley, Kitchen Cooked potato chips produced by Damien and Jerome Furukawa, and ice cream from Tropical Dreams are just a few of the local specialties we feature.

We're blessed to be located close to one of Hawai'i's richest agricultural areas. Aside from the island's world-renowned macadamia nuts and Kona coffee, of course, I bank on such talented people as Gary Kihara of Honaunau Produce, Russell Onedera of Onedera Produce in Waimea, and Harvy Sacarob of Sun Bear Produce, Inc. to provide us with an incredible bounty of fresh vegetables, fruits, herbs—you name it. These people are the best in their respective fields, and are more than just vendors—I'm fortunate to be able to call each of these remarkable, creative individuals my friends.

Take Harvy, for example. Along with his wife, Melinda, he began farming a sloping hillside up in Hookena Mauka about 12 years ago. A lot of people thought he was crazy at the time because the frequent mauka showers would regularly send water rushing down the hills, threatening to wash away crops and precious topsoil. It would never work, they told him. But instead of giving in, Harvy combined science with basic, back-breaking labor to prove the critics wrong. He received federal support to build a virgin dam at the top of the gardens to route the run-off rain water under, rather than through, his carefully terraced fields.

He struggled at first, but Harvy stuck to his dream, never compromising his commitment to all-organic farming, sustainable agriculture, and soil conservation principles. He doesn't use herbicides or pesticides on his food.

When I got together with some of the top chefs in Hawai'i to form Hawaii Regional Cuisine some years ago, I was glad to have had a hand in introducing them to Harvy's Sun Bear Produce and even hosted a get-together for Harvy and the group at the bowling alley. Basically, the quality of Harvy's produce speaks for itself, and today he supplies most of the key accounts in Kona, including Mauna Lani Resorts, Ritz Carlton, Hapuna Prince, Mauna Kea and the Royal Waikoloan.

To supply all of these clients and others, Harvy must make the most of the land he has to farm. Out of a total of five acres, he has about two acres of avocado and about two acres of produce, mostly baby lettuce. In that modest space he grows some 65,000 plants and further maximizes his land use by having a nearly equal number of seedlings sprouting in pots. When he harvests a bed on any given morning, it's cleaned up and replanted with one-month-old plants by the next morning. Through such careful management, his few acres produce as much as more than twice as many acres normally would. The bottom line to us, his customers, is that Sun Bear's produce is sweet and tender, has excellent color and texture, and is consistently available.

The last time I visited Harvy, he was experimenting with a gadget that emits special sounds. The sound waves vibrate the plant and open up the plant cells, he explained to me. Then, when he applies his seaweed nutrient to the plants, it is absorbed deeper, and seven times faster than without the sound. He said the plants grow faster, stronger and are more resistant to bugs. Don't laugh, I saw his test plots with my own eyes, and the plants treated with the sound were much bigger and better than those that weren't.

Harvy's not content to cruise on his success; he's always trying to improve what he's got, and I respect that a lot. Hey, better production, healthier and tastier plants, increased shelf life—he's making things better for all of us.

SPICY LAMB SALAD

SERVES 1

8   oz. boneless leg of lamb
1   Tbsp. oil
flour tortilla
assorted salad greens
cold cooked Japanese soba
    noodles, or angel hair pasta,
    cooked and chilled
salad dressing of your choice

This is a throwback to using miscuts of the whole lamb. Lamb is known for leg of lamb, rack of lamb, and lamb chops, but there are still other cuts left over that can be utilized, and this is one way of using some of them. You add spices and herbs and cook it real quick and it comes out tasty and tender. It's very healthy and very easy to prepare. It has become a very popular salad at our restaurant.

GARNISHES:
    cucumber, daikon, and
    radish strips
2 or 3 sprigs of fresh Chinese
    parsley or 1 or 2 sprigs fresh
    Thai basil
3   cucumber slices
3   tomato wedges
3   peeled orange segments

**MARINADE
FOR LAMB:**
1/4   cup leeks, scallions,
    or green onions, minced
1   clove garlic, minced
1-1/2 Tbsp. light salad oil
1/2   tsp. salt
1   Tbsp. shoyu
1-1/2 Tbsp. sherry
1/2   Tbsp. sugar
    white pepper to taste
1/4   tsp. sesame oil
1   Tbsp. ginger, minced
1   Tbsp. Chinese parsley,
    minced
2   fresh small red chili peppers

CUT lamb into strips about 1/2 inch wide by 1/4 inch thick by 1-1/2 inch long. Combine marinade ingredients and blend well. Remove 1 or 2 tablespoons of marinade and set aside for use later.

Marinate lamb for 5 to 10 minutes. Remove from marinade and set aside.

Cook soba noodles according to package directions, rinse in cold water, drain, add marinade you set aside earlier, mix well, and place in fridge for 20 to 30 minutes, or until chilled.

Deep-fry a flour tortilla until golden brown, then drain on paper towels, and set aside.

Prepare garnishes by thinly slicing with a potato peeler strips of cucumber, white daikon, radish, or vegetables of your choice. Place the strips in ice water for a few minutes to crisp. Wash and spin-dry salad greens. Set aside.

When everything is ready, quickly stir-fry lamb strips in 1 tablespoon. of hot oil (or more, as needed) in wok on high heat, for about 2 minutes. You don't want to overcook lamb, yet you want it to be hot when served.

Build the salad by placing the deep-fried tortilla on a plate, adding a handful or two of salad greens, topping with noodles, then lamb, then cucumber, daikon, and radish strips or garnishes of your choice. Lastly, place the sprigs of Chinese parsley or basil on top. Place the round cucumber slices, tomato wedges, and orange segments around edge of plate and enjoy with your choice of dressing.

HAWAIIAN BARBECUED SHRIMP SALAD WITH PAPAYA/PINEAPPLE MARMALADE

SERVES 4

This is one of my all-time most popular recipes. It's also very simple to make.

1 lb. jumbo shrimp (16-20 count)

4 flour tortillas

8-12 oz. Japanese somen noodles

1 medium head iceberg lettuce, finely julienned

1 cup bean sprouts

1 grated carrot

2 radishes, thinly sliced

2 cups napa cabbage or won bok, finely chopped

1/2 cup long strips green onions, diagonally sliced

4-8 wedges of fresh pineapple

4-8 wedges of fresh papaya

4-8 sprigs of Chinese parsley for garnish

dollops of *Papaya/Pineapple Marmalade*

MARINADE:

1/3 cup oil

2 Tbsp. *shoyu*

2 Tbsp. Chinese parsley, chopped

1 tsp. fresh ginger, minced

1 Tbsp. garlic, minced

1-1/2 tsp. sugar

1/4 tsp. red pepper flakes, or 1 fresh hot chili pepper, seeded and chopped

1 tsp. sesame oil

RINSE shrimp. Cut the top shell, but not all the way through because you're going to leave the shell on for a festive look. Peel shell from shrimp like a fan, leaving shell and tail attached at tail end. Devein shrimp. Combine marinade ingredients and blend well. Remove 4 tablespoons of marinade and set aside to mix with noodles. Marinate shrimp for 30 minutes.

Deep-fry flour tortillas and drain on paper towels. Set aside. Cook noodles according to package directions, rinse, drain, and mix with 4 tablespoons of marinade, then place in fridge until chilled, about 20 to 30 minutes.

In a large bowl combine lettuce, bean sprouts, grated carrot, sliced radishes, chopped *napa* cabbage, green onions, and mix well. Cut fresh pineapple and papayas into wedges, removing core and seeds.

When everything is ready, place shrimp on barbecue or under broiler and cook for 3 to 5 minutes, turning once.

Build each salad by first placing deep-fried tortilla on plate, adding a couple handfuls of colorful salad mix, then chilled somen noodles, then 1/4 of shrimp on top, and garnishing with a sprig or two of Chinese parsley.

Place the wedges of pineapple and papaya around the edge of plate, alternating with dollops of *Papaya/Pineapple Marmalade*.

I like my *Creamy Oriental* dressing with this salad, but you can use the dressing of your choice.

PAPAYA/PINEAPPLE MARMALADE:

1/2 cup papaya, diced

1/2 cup pineapple, diced

3 Tbsp. sugar

In saucepan cook fruit and sugar for 20 minutes. Serve warm, or cold.

You can't get much simpler than this: fresh whole shrimp with shells and heads on, marinated, then cooked quickly on the hibachi. Throw the shrimp on top of salad greens and marinated soba noodles and, man, you got a winner.

With 32 *Sam Choy*

ORIENTAL MACADAMIA NUT CHICKEN SALAD WITH FRIED NOODLES

SERVES 4

4	boneless chicken breasts (8 oz. each)
2	Tbsp. oil
	enough oil for deep-fat frying
1-oz.	package rice noodles
12	won ton wrappers, cut into strips and deep-fried
1	medium head iceburg lettuce, shredded
10	Chinese parsley sprigs, coarsely chopped
2	cups napa cabbage or wonbok, finely chopped
1	cup bean sprouts
1	cup red bell pepper, julienned
1	cup yellow bell pepper, julienned
1/2	cup green onions, thinly sliced (diagonally)
1	medium carrot, grated
6	radishes, thinly sliced
1	cup whole macadamia nuts
4	whole Chinese parsley sprigs, for garnish
1	head leaf lettuce, divided into leaves, for salad bed

MARINADE FOR CHICKEN:

1	cup shoyu
1	cup oil
4	Tbsp. mirin
1	tsp. sesame oil
4	Tbsp. Chinese parsley, minced
2	Tbsp. garlic, minced
2	Tbsp. ginger, minced
1	tsp. salt
1/2	tsp. white pepper
2	Tbsp. green onions, thinly sliced
4	Tbsp. cornstarch
3	tsp. brown sugar

Take a piece of chicken, marinate it, cover it with macadamia nuts, deep-fat fry it, or pan fry it, and serve it with fried noodles on mixed salad greens and one of our signature dressings, and you have yourself a surprisingly elegant, simple-to-prepare, and very satisfying salad.

COMBINE and blend all marinade ingredients, except for cornstarch and brown sugar, which you will first mix together then add to marinade ingredients. Add chicken and marinate for 1 to 2 hours in fridge.

Heat oil to 350 degrees. Drop rice noodles in oil and remove as soon as they puff up. (Don't brown them.) Drain on paper towels and break into bite-sized pieces when cool. Set aside.

Cut won ton wrappers into strips and deep-fry until golden brown in same oil you used for rice noodles. Drain on paper towels and set aside.

As soon as everything else is done and iceberg lettuce and other vegetables are sliced, chopped, and refrigerated, you can cook the chicken. Fry in 2 tablespoons oil, with skin on, until golden brown. Start on high heat, then finish on medium. After you turn the heat down, you can baste chicken with marinade. Continue basting, using about 1/2 cup of marinade in all, until liquid is absorbed and chicken is nicely browned. When done, let cool to room temperature and cut into strips.

Toss lettuce, cabbage, bean sprouts, and vegetables together with chicken and bite-sized pieces of rice noodles in mixing bowl. Add half of macadamia nuts and half of fried won ton strips, and toss with salad, reserving remaining nuts and won ton strips for garnish.

Arrange on individual salad plates on a bed of your favorite leaf lettuce. Use 1/4 of remaining macadamia nuts, 1/4 of remaining fried won ton strips, and a sprig of Chinese parsley to garnish each salad.

Serve with your choice of dressing. I especially like the *Sweet and Sour Cucumber Vinaigrette* with this particular salad. (For dressing recipe, see *Sam's Signature Salad Dressings* at end of salad section.)

• LEMON-PEPPER MAHIMAHI FILLET SALAD

SERVES 1

This gives you an opportunity to use something that's out there on the store shelf and blend it with indigenous fish to produce a real idiot-proof, world-class dish that doesn't take all day to prepare.

3 mahimahi fillets (2 oz. each)
2 Tbsp. olive oil
  lemon-pepper seasoning
1 or 2 handfuls of assorted salad greens, tossed with sauce
1 small package bean threads
  sprig or two of fresh basil, for garnish
1 Tbsp. green onions, finely sliced, for garnish

SAUCE FOR SALAD GREENS AND NOODLES:

1/2 cup oil
1/2 cup shoyu
1 tsp. sesame oil
2 Tbsp. mirin
1 Tbsp. garlic, minced
1 Tbsp. ginger, minced
1/2 tsp. salt
1/4 tsp. white pepper
1-1/2 tsp. brown sugar

LIGHTLY sprinkle fish with lemon-pepper seasoning and set aside while preparing rest of salad. (You want to cook the fish after everything else is ready so you can serve it hot.) Combine all sauce ingredients and blend well.

Place one package of bean threads in boiling water and boil until soft, about 5 minutes. Place in sieve, rinse with cold water and drain. Place on cutting board and cut into 1-inch lengths. Mix 2 to 3 tablespoons of sauce with about 3 ounces of cooked noodles, then chill, or let remain at room temperature, whichever you prefer.

Toss salad greens with 1/2 cup of sauce.

When everything is ready, quickly sear fish that you've lightly sprinkled with lemon-pepper on high heat in 2 tablespoons of olive oil until rare, or medium rare. For a low-fat variation, broil fish, but don't overcook.

Place lettuces in bowl with noodles on top, fish on top of that, and basil sprigs and green onions to top it all off.

You may find you don't need dressing, (the sauce tossed with the lettuce and noodles makes it very tasty), though I like to serve the *Wasabi Vinaigrette* with it because of the nice flavor contrasts.

BROILED GARLIC GARLIC CHICKEN BREAST SALAD

SERVES 1

In Asia, people like the dark meat of the chicken better than the white; they consider it more moist and flavorful; while in America, people seem to like the white meat better. To me, chicken breast can be kind of dry and boring, so I like to come up with ways to make it more interesting. I find that marinating it in garlic gives it a lot of flavor and seals in the juices.

1   **8-oz. chicken breast, boneless, with or without skin**

1   **Kau orange, or sweet navel orange, peeled and segmented**

1   **medium tangerine, peeled and segmented**

1/2 **fresh papaya, diced**

1/2 **cup fresh mango, or fresh pineapple, diced**

1 or 2 **handfuls of spring mix greens**

Creamy Oriental **Dressing**

a few edible flowers for garnish

MARINADE:

1   **Tbsp. garlic, minced**

1/2 **tsp. salt**

3   **Tbsp. sweet vermouth**

3   **Tbsp. melted butter**

1   **tsp. cracked peppercorns**

1   **tsp. Chinese parsley, chopped**

1   **Tbsp. green onions, thinly sliced**

MARINATE chicken breast one whole day in refrigerator. Mix fruits together and chill.

In a mixing bowl, toss salad greens and fruit together with enough *Creamy Oriental Dressing* to coat. (For *Creamy Oriental Dressing* recipe, see *Sam's Signature Salad Dressings* following this section.)

Grill or broil chicken breast, slice into strips, and place on top of salad, skin side up.

Garnish with edible nasturtiums and orchids, other edible flowers, or colorful garnish of your choice.

LASAGNA-STYLE HIBACHI TOFU SALAD

SERVES 2

This is a fun salad which has nothing to do with lasagna, other than using tofu in a lasagna-like layered fashion.

Basically, I came up with this as a different way to serve tofu. It's unique, but simple, and people really enjoy it. Stacking it seemed like something fun and interesting to do, and the marinade gives it a lot of flavor.

1   package tofu
4   Tbsp. olive oil
1/2   cup zucchini, julienned
1/2   cup sweet onions, julienned
1/2   cup carrots, julienned
1/2   cup red bell peppers, julienned
1/2   cup yellow bell peppers, julienned
1/2   cup bean sprouts
1/2   cup shiitake mushrooms, sliced
salt and pepper to taste
1-2   handfuls spring mix greens
Ginger Pesto, as garnish
Creamy Oriental Dressing
     and *Wasabi Vinaigrette*

MARINADE:

2   cloves garlic, minced
1-1/2 cups shoyu
1   cup sugar
1/4   cup fresh ginger, minced
2   Tbsp. green onions, thinly sliced
1   Tbsp. Chinese parsley
1   tsp. sesame oil
1/8   tsp. white pepper

DRAIN tofu and slice the whole block lengthwise into 3 equal sections then marinate for 1 to 2 hours. Prepare coals in hibachi.

In wok or sauté pan, heat 4 tablespoons olive oil until very hot, but not smoking. Add julienned vegetables, bean sprouts, and mushrooms and stir-fry for 2 to 3 minutes, until just wilted. Season with salt and pepper to taste. Add a handful or two of spring mix greens, cook another minute, and remove quickly from wok.

Remove tofu from marinade, cook on hibachi over hot coals about 2 or 3 minutes on each side, then remove from heat.

Put a small amount of stir-fried vegetables on salad plate, place 1 slice of tofu on top of vegetables, put a layer of vegetables on tofu, and continue alternating tofu and vegetables until you finish with a layer of vegetables on top.

Garnish with *Ginger Pesto* and drizzle dressing over each layer, either *Creamy Oriental* or *Wasabi Vinaigrette*, or both. (For dressing recipes, see *Sam's Signature Salad Dressings* following this section).

GINGER PESTO:

1/2   cup oil
1/2   tsp. salt
1/4   cup ginger, minced
1/4   cup green onions, minced
1/4   cup lightly packed Chinese parsley, minced
1/8   tsp. white pepper

In a small saucepan, heat oil, add salt and cook for 2 to 3 minutes. Cool. Stir in ginger, green onions, Chinese parsley, and white pepper.

POACHED FISH SALAD
WITH HONEY/LIME VINAIGRETTE

SERVES 1

Poaching fish is real simple and a good way to avoid oils and fats in cooking. The secret is to make the poaching water very flavorful so that it imparts a good flavor to the fish. The honey lime vinaigrette has both sweetness and tartness and adds a wonderful taste to this dish.

1 6-7-oz. fillet of opakapaka, red snapper, mahimahi, ono, or salmon
1 or 2 handfuls assorted salad greens
1/2 cup fresh tomato, diced
2 Tbsp. sweet onion, diced
2 Tbsp. green onions, sliced thin
pinch of sea salt

GARNISHES:
3 round orange slices
3 round tomato slices
1 sprig fresh dill

POACHING WATER:
2 cups water
1 cup white wine
1/2 cup carrots, diced
1/2 cup onions, diced
1/2 cup celery, diced
juice of 1/2 lemon
1/2 tsp. salt
1/4 tsp. cracked pepper

WHILE bringing poaching water to a boil, place salad greens on plate, combine diced tomato, sweet onion, green onion, and pinch of sea salt, blend well and place this lomi lomi mixture on greens.

Submerge fish completely in simmering poaching water, cover, and cook gently at a low simmer 5 to 8 minutes, maximum, for a single 6- to 7-ounce fillet. Increase cooking time slightly for larger portions, but don't overcook.

Place fish on tomato/onion mixture, garnish around edges with tomato and orange slices, top with sprig of fresh dill, and serve with Honey/Lime Vinaigrette.

HONEY/LIME VINAIGRETTE
2 Tbsp. honey
1 Tbsp. vinegar
juice from one medium lime
1 tsp. lime zest
1 Tbsp. fresh parsley, chopped
salt and white pepper to taste
1-1/2 Tbsp. light salad oil

Whisk together until well blended.

SCALLOPS AND SPINACH WITH GINGER PESTO

SERVES 1

This was inspired by the Caesar Salad and all those other great salads that are actually meals in themselves. Poached or pan-fried scallops combine nicely with the delicate flavor of spinach and are spiced up with ginger pesto. This salad has all sorts of textures and flavors giving every bite an exciting taste.

6	Sea scallops, 30-40 count
2	Tbsp. olive oil
6	oz. spinach (fresh is best), chopped
1/4	red bell pepper, sliced
2	mushrooms, sliced
1	oz. Parmesan cheese, grated
	salt and pepper to taste
1	8-in. flour tortilla, deep-fried

GINGER PESTO:

1/2	cup oil
1/2	tsp. salt
1/4	cup ginger, minced
1/4	cup green onions, minced
1/4	cup lightly packed Chinese parsley, minced
1/8	tsp. white pepper

HEAT oil in small saucepan, add salt and cook for 2 to 3 minutes. Cool. Stir in pesto ingredients and blend well. Marinate scallops in pesto sauce for 20 to 30 minutes, maximum.

After removing scallops from marinade, sear quickly in 2 tablespoons hot oil in wok on high heat until medium rare, 3 minutes, maximum—don't overcook. In mixing bowl, toss scallops together with spinach, red bell pepper, mushrooms, Parmesan cheese and pesto sauce. Season with salt and pepper, to taste.

Arrange mixture on deep-fried tortilla, or bed of leaf lettuce, and top with your favorite garnish.

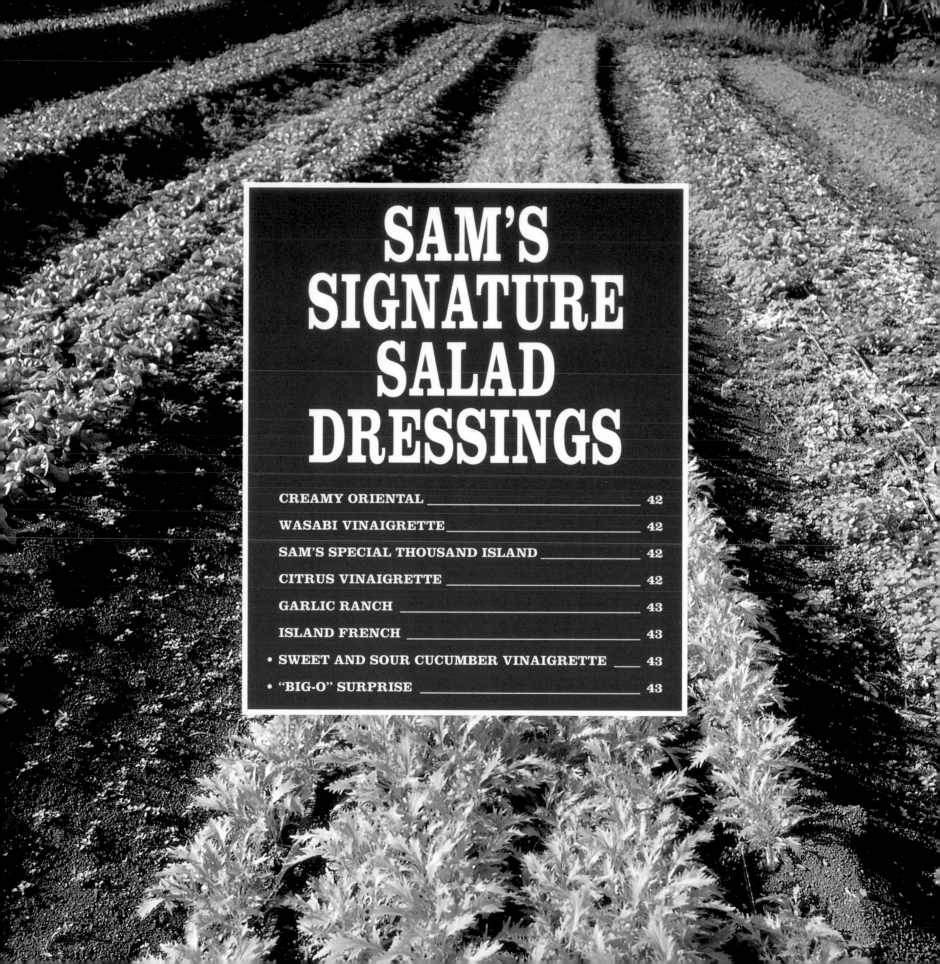

SAM'S SIGNATURE SALAD DRESSINGS

CREAMY ORIENTAL

MAKES 3 CUPS

3	cups mayonnaise
1/2	cup shoyu
3/4	cups sugar
1/4	tsp. white pepper
1-1/2	Tbsp. black sesame seeds
1	Tbsp. sesame oil

Whisk all ingredients together until well blended. If it's too thick you can whisk in a little water, a few drops at a time, until you get the consistency you like.

This is one of our own inventions and a real hit at our restaurant. I want to share it, because I always enjoy sharing a good thing—it makes me feel good. It's a very simple recipe, using some basic ingredients that you wouldn't normally think of putting together. It goes really well with all our marinated-fish salads, adding another layer of interesting flavors.

WASABI VINAIGRETTE

MAKES 3 CUPS

2	cups freshly squeezed orange juice
2	Tbsp. sesame seeds
3	Tbsp. sugar
1/2	cup oil
3	Tbsp. vinegar
2	Tbsp. shoyu
	salt to taste
2	Tbsp. wasabi

Mix all ingredients together and blend well.

Certain salads need spicing up to reach their peak. Wasabi adds a whole different flavor. I knew it was real popular with sushi and sashimi, so I wanted to play with it in a vinaigrette where people would notice it and have it wake up their taste buds, but where it wouldn't be overpowering.

SAM'S SPECIAL THOUSAND ISLAND

MAKES 3-1/2 CUPS

2	cups mayonnaise
1/2	cup half and half
4	tsp. sweet pickle relish, drained
4	Tbsp. chili sauce
1/2	Tbsp. black sesame seeds
1/2	tsp. dried red pepper flakes
	white pepper to taste
2	hard cooked eggs, chopped
1/2	cup tofu, diced

Combine first seven ingredients and mix well, then fold in tofu and chopped eggs.

Thousand Island dressing is very basic and easy to make, but I like to make things different. I add tofu and hard-boiled eggs and leave the ingredients chunky, almost as if the dressing is a salad in itself. When blended with a salad, it makes it seem special, something out of the ordinary.

CITRUS VINAIGRETTE

MAKES 2 QUARTS

1	pint light salad oil
1	cup balsamic vinegar
1	cup fresh orange juice salt and pepper to taste
2	Tbsp. fresh basil, chopped
2	Tbsp. Chinese parsley, chopped
2	Tbsp. sugar (or more, to taste)
1	tsp. dry mustard

Combine all ingredients except oil. Whisk until sugar is completely dissolved and mixture is thoroughly blended. Gradually add oil while continuing to whisk. Readjust seasoning with salt, pepper, and sugar. It is important to dissolve all the sugar before getting the true taste. Keep whisking until mixed well.

Ka'u on the Big Island produces a navel orange that is exceptionally sweet and juicy. I like to take that orange and extract its juice to make a tasty vinaigrette. It adds a real natural flavor, yet is so delicate it doesn't overwhelm the flavors of the salad greens and vegetables—you can still taste those flavors—the dressing simply enhances their freshness.

GARLIC RANCH

MAKES 1 QUART

3	cloves garlic, minced
1/2	cup onions, minced
1/4	cup sugar
1/4	cup red wine vinegar
1/2	cup olive oil
2	cups mayonnaise
	salt and pepper to taste
2	tsp. dry mustard
1	Tbsp. fresh oregano, minced
1	Tbsp. fresh basil, chopped

Combine all ingredients and whisk until thoroughly blended. Chill.

This creamy, rich dressing makes eating salad a very memorable experience. I love to use garlic in my cooking because it spices up and brings out the flavor of whatever you put it on. And ranch is a very versatile dressing—it's used not only on salads, but on sandwiches and for dips as well.

ISLAND FRENCH

MAKES 1 QUART

1	tsp. lime juice
1	cup ketchup
1	cup cider vinegar
1/4	cup light salad oil
3/4	cup sugar
	white pepper and salt to taste
1	tsp. dry mustard
1/2	medium-sized Maui onion, finely minced
1	clove garlic, minced

Mix all ingredients except oil in a blender on purée setting for about 1 minute, then begin adding oil slowly. Readjust seasonings and blend for about 2 minutes after adding all the oil. Total blending time will be 3 to 4 minutes. Refrigerate.

This is a "local-style" take on a very classic dressing. I think you'll enjoy it.

• SWEET AND SOUR CUCUMBER VINAIGRETTE

MAKES 2 CUPS

1	cup white vinegar
1/2	cup water
3/4	cup sugar
	pinch salt
	white pepper to taste
1	cup cucumbers, very thinly sliced
1/2	Tbsp. ginger, grated

Blend until sugar dissolves. Chill.

This was inspired by a simple Asian dipping sauce that goes very nicely with crispy won ton or spring rolls. I've just added a few more ingredients and turned it into a vinaigrette for salad. It goes really well with my spicy lamb or poached fish salad.

• BIG "O" SURPRISE

MAKES 2 CUPS

1	12-oz. can V-8 vegetable juice
1	tsp. onion, minced
1	clove garlic, minced
1	tsp. parsley, chopped
1	tsp. Chinese parsley, chopped
1/2	cup green onion, thinly sliced
1	Tbsp. vinegar
1	Tbsp. lime juice
1	Tbsp. each, red and yellow bell pepper, minced

Combine all ingredients and mix well. Chill.

You'll be surprised how good this tastes.

This dressing has no fat at all, that's why I call it the "Big O." It's a great dressing not only for people watching their weight, but also for people looking for something different to put on their salad. It's basically a salsa and is very versatile; you can fold it into rice, use as a topping, or whatever your imagination comes up with.

SOUPS

WHEN YOU'RE HUNGRY BEAN SOUP

SERVES 8 TO 10

1 cup dried kidney beans

1 cup dried navy beans

1 cup black beans

1 or 2 lbs. ham chunks

1-1/2 cups tomato purée

1 qt. chicken stock

water, as needed

2 cups onion chunks

2 cups carrot chunks

2 cups celery chunks

2 cups potato chunks

1-1/2 cups Chinese parsley, chopped

1 package Portuguese sausage, sliced and cooked

2 ears fresh corn, cut into 2-in. sections

salt and pepper to taste

SORT and rinse beans, soak overnight. Drain. Place in stockpot with ham, tomato purée, chicken stock, and enough water to cover.

Bring to a boil, reduce heat, cover, and simmer until meat and beans are tender. Add onion, carrot, celery and potato chunks, Chinese parsley, and Portuguese sausage and simmer until vegetables are cooked. Add corn and simmer an additional 5 minutes. Season with salt and pepper.

I really enjoy making soup because everything is in one pot and that makes it easy. Good soup is always good, you can't mess with it, but soup is only as good as the stock, and it's best to make the stock from scratch, using bones and fresh ingredients. You can make a big batch ahead of time, then freeze it in ziplock bags so you'll always have some on hand. Canned broth is okay, but the canning process changes the flavor, as does the drying process for bullion. Like in all cooking, for the best flavor, use the freshest ingredients. This bean soup is one of my favorites. It's hard to beat.

CREAM OF CARROT

SERVES 4 TO 6

1 lb. carrots, grated

1/2 cup Maui onions,
      or sweet onions, minced

3 Tbsp. butter

1 qt. chicken stock

1/2 cup cooked rice

1 tsp. sugar

salt and pepper to taste

2 cups heavy cream
   Garlic Croutons
   (recipe follows)

SAUTÉ carrots with onions in butter. When tender, add chicken stock and rice. Adjust seasoning with sugar, salt, and pepper. Simmer for 15 minutes, then add heavy cream and cook for 5 more minutes. Serve with *Garlic Croutons*.

GARLIC CROUTONS:

2 white bread slices

1 Tbsp. melted butter

1 Tbsp. olive oil

1/2 tsp. garlic, minced

Remove crust and cut bread into cubes. Drizzle bread cubes with melted butter and oil, then toss with garlic. Place on cookie sheet and bake in 325-degree oven for about 6 to 8 minutes, or until brown. Makes about 1 cup.

This recipe is the result of working closely with local farmers. Fresh carrots are totally different from what you get at the store, so much more juice comes out when you grate them, and they have that great fresh taste and are so much sweeter. They make for a very colorful and flavorful soup, and one that is unique.

SAM CHOY'S SOUTHPOINT CHOWDER

SERVES 8

As more and more areas around the Hawaiian chain get fished out, we're finding that places like Southpoint on the Big Island, Nihoa on Kauai, and the windward coasts of every island still harbor an abundance of fish. What is saving those places is the roughness of the weather. People don't want to chance it in small dinghies. The majority of fish we use in our restaurant are from Southpoint. It's really rough out there. You have to know what you're doing. It's where you find the real fishermen.

8	mussels
1	lb. firm white fish
1/4	lb. shrimp
1/4	lb. scallops
6	strips bacon, diced
1	onion, minced
3	stalks celery, minced
1	potato, peeled and diced
1	sweet potato, peeled and diced
2	cups fish stock (recipe follows)
1/2	cup creamed corn
1/2	cup fresh corn kernels
	salt and white pepper to taste
	Pinch of fresh thyme
2	cups heavy cream
	Chopped parsley as garnish

RINSE mussels and cut in half. Cube fish. Peel and devein shrimp. Set seafood aside. In a heavy stockpot, fry bacon, onions, and celery until onions are translucent. Add potatoes and fish stock. Cover and simmer until potatoes are cooked. Add fish, mussels, shrimp, scallops, salt, white pepper, and thyme. Cover and simmer until fish is done. Add creamed corn and corn kernels. Stir in heavy cream and heat thoroughly, but don't boil. Garnish with parsley.

FISH STOCK:

2-1/2	lbs. fish bones, rinsed
1	cup white wine
4	stalks celery, chopped
1	carrot, chopped
1	onion, chopped
1	Tbsp. fresh ginger root, minced
1-1/2	tsp. sea salt
1/2	tsp. white pepper

Place fish bones in a large pot. Add white wine, vegetables, ginger, salt, pepper, and enough water to cover bones. Bring to a boil. Reduce heat and simmer for 25 minutes. Strain. Fish stock should be used when fresh.

CREAMY MACADAMIA NUT SOUP
SERVES 6

1   qt. chicken broth

3   cups macadamia nuts, chopped

3/4   cup onion, minced

6   Tbsp. butter

6   Tbsp. flour

4   cups heavy cream

salt and white pepper to taste

chopped parsley, for garnish

COARSELY chop nuts and place in a saucepan (reserve a small amount to sprinkle on finished soup as garnish). Add onions and chicken stock. Bring to a boil, reduce heat to simmer, cover and cook for about 15 minutes.

In another pan, melt butter and stir in flour. Cook, stirring with a wooden spatula, over high heat for 2 minutes—do not brown.

Add to simmering nut/stock mixture, fold in cream and let simmer for 3 to 4 minutes. Add salt and pepper to taste. Garnish with chopped parsley and a sprinkle of chopped macadamia nuts.

In 1994, when I was invited to go pick macadamia nuts for the first time after living on the Big Island for five years, I quickly found out how hard and how backbreaking it is to go and harvest those little buggers. It's worth it, though. Every bite lightens you up. I don't mean in weight, but in spirit. When you eat them it's like a kid in a candy store—you just want to eat more and more, and you get all excited about it. This soup catches some of that excitement.

MY DAD'S ONG CHOY AND PORK SOUP

SERVES 6 TO 8

This is a great soup when you don't have much time to spend in the kitchen.

2   **cups shiitake mushrooms, sliced**
1/4   **lb. lean pork**
1/4   **cup raw shrimp, peeled and deveined**
1/4   **cup celery, julienned**
1/4   **cup scallions, julienned**
1   **bunch ong choy, cut into 2-in. sections**
salt and white pepper to taste
8   **cups chicken stock**
1   **piece ginger, about 3/4 in. by 3/4 in.**

CUT pork into slivers. Bring chicken stock to a boil and add ginger, pork, celery, and scallions. Reduce heat and simmer, covered, for 10 to 15 minutes. Add ong choy, mushrooms, and shrimp and cook about 3 minutes. Adjust seasoning with salt and pepper to taste.

One of the exciting things about growing up in my family was playing outside and then coming in and smelling that unforgettable aroma of my dad's soup simmering on the stove. It's delicious and very simple to make.

TARO CORN CHOWDER

SERVES 8 TO 10

2   **lbs. taro, diced small**
3/4   **cup salt pork or bacon**
3/4   **cup onions, diced small**
3/4   **cup celery, diced small**
1-1/2 **cups flour**
1   **qt. chicken stock**
2   **cups creamed corn**
4   **cups whole kernel corn**
2   **pts. heavy cream**
salt and white pepper to taste

PLACE taro in pot, cover with water, bring to a boil, reduce heat and simmer until tender, then set aside. Sauté bacon or chopped salt pork with onions and celery until onions are translucent. Add flour and cook until flour turns into a blond roux. Add chicken stock, creamed corn, whole kernel corn, taro, and heavy cream. Adjust seasoning with salt and pepper. Let simmer 6 to 8 minutes, then serve hot. Great on a cold night.

This is one of my favorite soups. Taro is what they make poi out of. A lot of people turn their noses up at poi because they think it's like eating wallpaper paste. But when I cook this chowder and sneak the taro in, you should see them go, "Oh, wow! What is this? It's so good!!!" I get a kick out of telling them it's taro.

PUMPKIN BISQUE

SERVES 8 TO 10

The only time I used to use pumpkin was in pumpkin pie. But because I like to innovate, I've enjoyed taking something that's noted only for one thing, like pie, and then using it in a very different way. It shows how versatile a vegetable or fruit can be. Because you're adding an entirely different set of spices, this soup doesn't taste anything like pumpkin pie. It has a rich, creamy flavor that I know you will enjoy.

2	Tbsp. butter
1	Tbsp. garlic, minced
1	tsp. ginger, minced
1/2	cup celery, medium diced
3/4	cup carrots, medium diced
3/4	cup Maui onion, medium diced
1/2	cup green onions, medium diced
2	lbs. fresh pumpkin, cubed
3-1/2	qts. chicken stock
1	qt. heavy cream

salt and pepper to taste
fresh whipped cream, for garnish
ground cinnamon, for garnish

IN a large saucepan, sauté garlic, ginger, celery, carrots, onions, and green onions in butter. Add pumpkin and chicken stock. Bring to a boil, reduce heat and simmer until tender. Remove solids and purée in a blender while adding enough liquid to achieve the desired consistency. Return to pot. Add heavy cream and blend well. Heat until soup is hot, but not boiling. Adjust seasoning with salt and pepper. Garnish with a spoonful of fresh whipped cream and a sprinkle of cinnamon.

BIG ISLAND AVOCADO BISQUE

SERVES 3 TO 6

2 or 3 large, ripe avocados,
    peeled and pitted
3/4   cup lime juice
2   cups chicken broth
3   cups heavy cream
2   Tbsp. Chinese parsley,
    minced
salt and pepper to taste

PLACE peeled avocados in large mixing bowl with lime juice, and whip with a wire whip until smooth and creamy. Season with salt and pepper. Slowly add the chicken broth, stirring to blend, then add the heavy cream. Fold in Chinese parsley. Chill. Be sure this soup is very cold before serving.

Optional: Garnish the top of each cup of soup with chilled, cooked Bay shrimp, Sam Choy Kona Cuisine style.

Many yards in Kona have avocado trees, and a lot of avocados hit the ground and either get eaten by wild pigs or turn into compost. I'm always experimenting with new ways to use this tasty and nutritious fruit so it doesn't go to waste. This delicious and unique bisque is just one result of that experimentation.

COLD PAPAYA, MANGO, AND POHA BERRY BISQUE

SERVES 4 TO 6

1   lb. mangoes
1-1/2   lbs. papayas
2   cups fresh Poha berries
    (Cape gooseberries)
2   cups pineapple juice
    (or enough to cover fruit)
1   large slice fresh ginger
1/2   cinnamon stick
4   grains allspice
3-4   black peppercorns
1/2   cup honey
lemon juice to taste
1   cup cornstarch mixed with
    1/2 cup water
    (for thickening, as needed)

**GARNISH
PER SERVING:**

2   tsp. sour cream
1/2   tsp. toasted macadamia
    nuts, chopped

PEEL, seed, and chop mangoes and papaya. Leave berries whole. Place fruit in saucepan, cover with pineapple juice, add spices and honey and simmer until fruit is tender. Discard cinnamon stick. Purée soup in blender until very smooth. Strain, if desired.

Return soup to simmer. If necessary, thicken by adding cornstarch mix a little at a time to simmering soup while stirring, until desired consistency is reached. Adjust the flavor with lemon juice. Chill thoroughly. Just before serving, garnish each portion with a dollop of sour cream and a sprinkling of toasted macadamia nuts.

I like to take overripe papaya, mango, and poha berries and blend them into a beautiful fruit bisque. It's a great way to utilize fruits that are too ripe, and it's also a way to use fruit that you have frozen. You can freeze any fruit. It's just not very appealing after it comes out of the freezer, so here is a way to use it that makes it look and taste very good.

LUAU COCONUT CRABMEAT WITH TARO

SERVES 8 TO 10

This recipe was inspired by our family method of making squid or chicken luau. You take Hawaiian taro leaf top, which is called luau, and cook it down to make Hawaiian spinach, and then blend it with coconut milk and taro and fresh crab meat. It makes a very, very good soup.

2	cups Maui onions, minced
1/2	cup butter
1	Tbsp. sugar
3	cups heavy cream
2	cups chicken stock
2	cups coconut milk
1-1/2	cups taro, diced (steam until tender, then dice)
2	lbs. fresh luau (taro) leaves, stems removed
2	cups crabmeat
	salt and pepper to taste
1-1/2	cups cornstarch mixed with 1/2 cup water, for thickening agent

RINSE luau leaves and boil 4 to 5 minutes, then rinse in cold water, strain, squeeze dry, and chop. In a large saucepan, sauté onions in butter, add sugar, and cook until onions look translucent. Add chicken stock, heavy cream, and taro. Simmer for about 5 minutes, stirring frequently. Stir in coconut milk, luau leaves, and crabmeat. When soup begins to simmer, thicken by adding cornstarch mixture very slowly, a little at a time while stirring, until you get the consistency you desire. Simmer until you can't taste the cornstarch. Adjust seasoning with salt and pepper.

This is my favorite soup because it's real fun both to make and to eat.

MAIN DISHES

ISLAND BRAISED
LAMB SHANKS

SERVES 6 TO 10

Home cooks don't usually think much about presentation, but when you arrange food artistically on the plate, it enhances the flavor. Even a T.V. dinner—if you take it out of the tin and put it on a plate and add a sprig of fresh parsley—it only takes a minute, but it really makes the food seem to taste better. It's like the presentation sets up your taste buds; if your eye sees something that looks good, you're going to enjoy it more. I like using a vertical presentation, which is sort of a "new wave" thing. Who says you have to serve pork chops the boring old traditional way with the mashed potatoes on one side and the vegetable on the other? Why not make eating more exciting and fun by putting the mashed potatoes in the middle of the plate, stir-fried vegetables on top of the potatoes, and the pork chops on top of that, with a colorful garnish to top it all off? The height makes it look elegant, and all the flavors blended together in every bite makes it taste real good.

3	lbs. lamb shanks
1/2	cup vegetable oil
4	cloves garlic, minced
8	cups chicken broth or stock (or enough to cover meat)
1/2	tsp. ground Five Star Spice
1/2	cup Chinese parsley
5	Tbsp. dry sherry
2	Tbsp. brown sugar
1	finger fresh ginger root, sliced
5	Tbsp. shoyu
1/2	cup onions, julienned
1/2	cup celery, julienned
1/2	cup red bell pepper, julienned
1/2	cup yellow bell pepper, julienned
4	Tbsp. cornstarch blended well with 3 Tbsp. water, for thickening

IN a large stockpot brown lamb shanks with garlic in 1/2 cup oil (reserving 4 tablespoons of oil for later use) until golden brown, about 6 to 8 minutes over medium-high heat. Cover meat with chicken broth, then add Five Star Spice, Chinese parsley, sherry, brown sugar, ginger, and shoyu. Bring to a boil on stove top, cover with foil or oven-proof lid and place in 350-degree oven. Braise for about 1 hour, or until tender.

Remove lamb and strain stock. Set stock and lamb aside and keep warm.

In a large skillet, heat 4 tablespoons oil over medium-high heat and stir-fry onions, celery, and peppers for about 2 or 3 minutes, then add stock and bring to a boil. While it's boiling, add cornstarch mixture and cook until thickened.

Arrange shanks nicely on a platter, and cover with vegetable/sauce mixture.

MARINATED LAMB LOIN

SERVES 4

2 to 3 lbs. boneless lamb loin,
     trimmed of fat

MARINADE:

2	Tbsp. shoyu
2	Tbsp. oil
1	Tbsp. Chinese parsley, minced
1	Tbsp. brown sugar
1	Tbsp. garlic, minced
1	Tbsp. shallots, minced
1	Tbsp. cracked black pepper
2	Tbsp. fresh thyme, rosemary, or basil (or combination)
1	tsp. salt

COMBINE marinade ingredients and massage into lamb. Let marinate for 4 to 6 hours in refrigerator.

Broil 4 to 6 minutes per side for medium rare, or to desired doneness.

Serve with *Pineapple/Papaya Marmalade*. (You will find this marmalade recipe under *Hawaiian Barbecue Shrimp Salad*.)

If you simply season a lamb loin with salt and pepper and some fresh herbs, it's going to be okay, but there's a big difference between okay and great. The marinating featured in this recipe is what makes the difference. To marinate lamb loin literally puts it in a different world. When you do it as I've suggested, it makes it much more fun and exciting.

ORIENTAL LAMB CHOPS WITH ROTELLI PASTA

SERVES 4 TO 6

2 or 3 lamb chops per serving
(8 to 18 chops total)

MARINADE:

1/2	cup shoyu
3/4	cup garlic, minced
1	Tbsp. fresh ginger, minced
2	cups brown sugar
1/2	tsp. chili flakes
1/2	cup basil, minced
1/2	cup Chinese parsley, minced
	salt to taste

I've been very blessed with this dish being so successful in our restaurant. Basically, I've taken Chinese methods and flavorings, added a twist, and come up with this award-winning recipe.

COMBINE marinade ingredients, massage into meat for 5 to 10 minutes, then let marinate 4 to 6 hours in refrigerator.

Broil to perfection (about 2 to 3 minutes per side for medium rare, or to your liking.)

ROTELLI PASTA:

2	Tbsp. butter
4	Tbsp. olive oil
1-1/2	Tbsp. garlic, minced
1	medium carrot, julienned
2	medium zucchini, julienned
2	cups shiitake mushrooms, julienned
1/2	cup Chinese parsley, coarsely chopped
12-oz.	bag rotelli, cooked according to package directions, drained
6	cups heavy cream
	salt and pepper to taste
3/4	cup grated Parmesan cheese

In a large saucepan, heat butter and olive oil over medium-high heat, cook garlic for about 1 minute, without browning, then add vegetables and stir-fry for 2 to 3 minutes. Add drained cooked pasta and stir-fry another minute. Add heavy cream, bring to a boil, then immediately reduce to a simmer. Adjust seasoning with salt and pepper. Just before serving fold in 3/4 cup Parmesan cheese and let cook 1 minute.

Serve in large pasta bowls with 2 or 3 *Oriental Lamb Chops* on top, garnished with sprigs of fresh basil.

CRUSTED PORK LOIN ROAST
SERVES 6

As you read through this cookbook you will notice that I almost always like to marinate meats and chicken, as well as certain seafoods, before cooking them. This adds interesting flavors and nice surprises. I've discovered that if you marinate prior to cooking, it doesn't overpower but adds subtle flavor that makes for a whole different world in eating. I don't usually marinate fish because I use only the freshest which has a very delicate flavor you don't want to cover up.

1   pork loin (3 lbs.), trimmed of fat

MARINADE:

1   cup shoyu
4   Tbsp. brown sugar
1   Tbsp. ginger, minced
1   Tbsp. garlic, minced
1/2 cup sherry

CRUST:

1-1/2 cups flour
4   whole eggs, beaten
3   cups panko
2   cups macadamia nuts, chopped
1/2 cup almonds, chopped

COMBINE all marinade ingredients and massage into pork for 8 to 10 minutes. Let marinate 2 to 3 hours in fridge.

Remove meat, blot off excess marinade, roll in flour, then in beaten egg, then in breading mixture of panko and nuts. Press breading firmly onto meat.

Place directly in roasting pan (no rack) and roast in 325-degree preheated oven for 45 minutes to 1 hour, or until interior temperature reaches 180 degrees on a meat thermometer.

No Need 'Fufu' Restaurant

People ask me why I operate such a simple-looking restaurant, located in an industrial area in Kona. They ask me if I don't want to open up a fancy establishment somewhere else. Well, I honestly don't. The physical trappings of fancy "fufu" restaurants—leather booths, chandeliers, crystal goblets—simply don't excite me. Personally, I think when people walk into a "fufu" restaurant, the first thing they tend to do is grab their behinds, because the immediate feeling is, "Hang on to your wallets, folks, here it comes!"

My tastes are simple. I want a place that's very clean, and I want to provide good service. I'm a fanatic on cleanliness. My dad always told me, "Son, always keep things very clean when you cook, because people eat food to nourish their bodies."

Beyond that, you have to let your food do the talking. What you put in front of people tells the real story—not gold-trimmed plates or dimmer switches that turn the lights down at a certain time of the evening.

Cooking is not like, say, construction, where they can put things you can't see behind a wall. An unscrupulous contractor could tell you, "We installed the finest gold cables in there, so I have to add another $1,500 to the original quote." Now, you aren't going to rip a hole in your wall to check if you really got gold cables, are you? With food, what's important is what's sitting in front of you. If the food's bad, it's bad. You can't hide it.

My goal is to create an atmosphere that's the opposite of a "fufu" restaurant's. I want a place where people can feel, "Ho, I'm so glad I came in shorts and T-shirt." I think about the hectic, stressful pace that people have to keep these days. We pick up the newspaper and it's filled with negative things—the economy, murders, bank robberies, corruption. When lunch or dinner time rolls around and people enter a really upscale restaurant, it's just an extension of the pace they've been keeping all day.

People need a place and a time in their day to really take their minds off of what they're doing. I believe what people want more and more is a good, local restaurant that features good, local flavors. I've tried to capture that feeling, so people can say, "Eh, let's go to Sam Choy's. Over there, you no need worry about nothing. No need dress up to go to Sam Choy's restaurant, but the food, hey, the food is just as good as you'll find anywhere else."

I truly believe that's the magic . . . that is the magic.

HALEIWA BARBECUED PORK RIBS

SERVES 4 TO 6

The reason we call this "Haleiwa Barbecued Pork Ribs" is that we used to go to Haleiwa Beach Park on Sunday drives and have barbecues. It was important that we always had the ribs all marinated and cooked ahead of time so we didn't have to spend all day cooking. We'd just throw them on the grill, brush them with sauce and, as soon as they heated through, we'd have a delicious, quick meal.

2   whole slabs pork ribs, cut into sections of 3 ribs each
enough water to cover ribs in stockpot
1/2   cup sea salt
4   cloves garlic, whole
1   finger fresh ginger, whole
2   green onions, whole

HALEIWA BARBECUE SAUCE:
1   tsp. red chili flakes
2   cans (15 oz.) tomato sauce
2   cups brown sugar
1/2   cup vinegar
1/2   cup honey
2   cups onion, minced
2   tsp. liquid smoke
2   tsp. chili powder
1   tsp. coarsely cracked black pepper
2   Tbsp. steak sauce
1/2   tsp. dry mustard
1   cinnamon stick
1   cup canned crushed pineapple
1   Tbsp. garlic, minced

PLACE ribs in stockpot and cover with water. Start with 1/2 cup sea salt and keep adding until water tastes salty, then add garlic, ginger, and green onions. Bring to a boil. Reduce heat and let simmer 45 minutes to 1 hour, or until ribs are tender.

While ribs are cooking, combine all barbecue sauce ingredients in a saucepan, bring to a boil, reduce heat and simmer 1 hour. Strain.

When ribs are tender, remove from stockpot and let cool. Brush with barbecue sauce and grill over hot coals on a hibachi until heated through. Baste the ribs with barbecue sauce as they cook.

STUFFED PORK CHOPS WITH MUSHROOM PAN GRAVY

SERVES 4

This is a great meal to serve to guests, because it's very easy to prepare, yet it looks like you went to a lot of trouble and spent a lot of time in the kitchen. It seems like something really special. And if you're in a hurry, you can stuff the pork chops the night before. When you serve them on a platter with mashed potatoes and pan gravy, your guests will think you're a genius.

4	center-cut pork chops (8 oz. each and 1-1/2 in. thick)
3/4	cup flour
4	Tbsp. oil
3	cups chicken broth
1	cup onions, julienned
1	cup mushrooms, sliced
4	Tbsp. cornstarch mixed with
3 Tbsp. water, for thickening	
salt and pepper to taste	

STUFFING:

1/2	cup butter
1	medium onion, minced
6	strips bacon, chopped
1	celery stalk, minced
1/2	cup fresh spinach, chopped
1	medium apple, diced
2-1/2 cups chicken broth	
1/2	Tbsp. poultry seasoning
1/2	cup raisins (optional)
3	cups toasted croutons or stuffing mix
salt and pepper to taste	

TO prepare pork chops for stuffing, make a 2-inch-wide slit on edge of chop opposite the bone and cut into center, making a deep enough pocket to hold stuffing in the middle of each chop. Set aside.

To make stuffing, sauté minced onions, bacon, celery, spinach, and apples in butter until onions look translucent. Add chicken broth and poultry seasoning and bring to a boil. Add raisins and cook 3 minutes, or until soft. Remove from heat. Add croutons, or stuffing mix, stir, season with salt and pepper and set aside until cooled to room temperature.

Divide stuffing into four equal portions and stuff pork chops. Season stuffed chops with salt and pepper and dust with flour.

In a pan large enough to hold the 4 chops, heat oil on medium-high heat and brown the chops (about 2 to 3 minutes on each side), then reduce heat to medium. Add chicken broth, julienned onions, and mushrooms. Bring to a boil, then cover with foil, or an oven-proof lid, and bake in 350-degree oven for 35 to 40 minutes. Remove pork chops when done and keep warm while making pan gravy.

Place pan with drippings on medium heat and skim off fat. Bring to a boil, then reduce to simmer. Thicken with cornstarch/water mixture by adding gradually until gravy reaches the consistency you like.

This dish goes great with my *Garlic Mashed Potatoes.* (*See Sam's Favorite Side Dishes* section.)

STUFFED PORK LOIN WITH COUNTRY BEAN SAUCE

SERVES 4 TO 6

1   whole pork loin (3 lbs.)
2   tsp. garlic, minced
1/2   cup flour
3   Tbsp. olive oil
    alt and pepper to taste

STUFFING:

1/2   cup butter
1   medium onion, minced
6   strips bacon, chopped
1   celery stalk, minced
1/2   cup fresh spinach, chopped
1/2   cup mushrooms, chopped
1   medium apple, diced
3   cups chicken broth
1/2   Tbsp. poultry seasoning
1/2   cup raisins (optional)
4   cups toasted croutons or stuffing mix
1/2   cup macadamia nuts, chopped
salt and pepper to taste

COUNTRY BEAN SAUCE:

2 or 3   ham hocks
6   cups water
6   cups chicken stock or broth
1   can (15 oz.) kidney beans
2   cups tomato sauce
2   medium carrots, diced
4   stalks celery, diced
2   medium onions, diced
1/2   cup Chinese parsley, chopped
1/2   bunch watercress cut into 1-in. pieces
2   cloves garlic, minced
3   potatoes, peeled and diced
salt and pepper to taste

CUT a 2-inch-wide slit all through the middle of the whole loin, being careful not to exit sides. Set aside.

To make stuffing, sauté onions, bacon, celery, spinach, mushrooms, and apples in butter until onions look translucent. Add chicken broth and poultry seasoning and bring to a boil. Add raisins (if desired) and cook 3 minutes, or until soft. Remove from heat. Add croutons, or stuffing mix, and macadamia nuts. Stir, adjust seasoning with salt and pepper, and set aside until cooled to room temperature.

Stuff pork loin with cooled stuffing. Rub outside with salt and pepper and minced garlic. Roll in flour and brown well in olive oil. Roast in 350-degree oven for 35 to 40 minutes. After removing from oven, cool 10 to 15 minutes to make slicing easier.

Cover ham hocks with water and chicken broth and bring to a boil. Reduce heat, add garlic and simmer covered for 3 hours, or until ham hocks are tender. Add everything else and cook about 20 minutes more, or until vegetables are soft. Adjust seasoning with salt and pepper. If necessary to thicken, finely grate 1 raw potato into sauce for the last 5 minutes of cooking time.

This dish is best when served with my *Garlic Mashed Potatoes* (see *Sam's Favorite Side Dishes* section) in this manner:

Place a heaping spoonful or two of mashed potatoes on plate. Top with 1-1/2 cups of *Country Bean Sauce*, and 2 or 3 slices of stuffed pork loin. It's really good.

Pork loin is generally very dry because you have to cook pork until it's well done, and it's hard to keep it moist when you have to cook it so long. What I like to do is stuff it to maintain moisture and to add flavor. Then to top it off, I add Country Bean Sauce, which blends a lot of flavors all together and makes it just wonderful.

PORK CUTLET KOLOKO

SERVES 4

Because cutlets are thin, they're easy to dry out. I like to make sure the food I cook is moist. The way I look at it is you might as well not eat if you're going to dry something out. One of my secrets is to let the meat sit, covered, at room temperature for a few minutes so it warms up a little after being taken out of the fridge. This causes the muscles to relax so it will be juicier. Then you sear it real quick to seal in those juices. Try this with chicken, too. Just let it sit long enough to get the chill out, and it will cook quicker and be more tender, juicy, and flavorful.

1-1/2 lbs. pork loin, cut into
    12 cutlets (2 oz. each and
    about 3/8 in. thick)
salt and pepper to taste
1-1/2 cup flour (more or less as
    needed, for dusting)
1   whole onion
2   cups oil (or enough for
    deep-fat frying)
3   Tbsp. oil
Country Bean Sauce
    (see recipe under
    ***Stuffed Pork Loins*)**
Garlic Mashed Potatoes
    (see recipe under Sam's
    Favorite Side Dishes)
Sprigs of fresh Chinese
    parsley, for garnish

POUND cutlets flat with a wooden mallet. Lightly season with salt and pepper, dust with flour to coat, and set aside.

Slice an onion very thinly into circular slices and dust slices with flour. Heat oil to 350 degrees for deep-fat frying. Drop in onions and fry until golden brown, while moving around with tongs so slices don't stick together. If your deep-fat fryer is large enough, you can fry the onions in one batch, otherwise, just do a few at a time. Drain, and set aside. In a sauté pan heat 3 tablespoons oil on medium-high heat and sauté cutlets about 2 minutes on each side, or until brown.

The best way to serve them is on top of *Garlic Mashed Potatoes* smothered with *Country Bean Sauce.* Top the cutlets with the fried onions and a sprig of Chinese parsley for a great meal.

SWEET AND SOUR PINEAPPLE PORK

SERVES 4

1	lb. lean pork	**SWEET AND SOUR**	
1	Tbsp. shoyu	**SAUCE:**	
1	Tbsp. sweet vermouth	1/2	cup tomato catsup
1	tsp. garlic, minced	1/2	cup vinegar
1	tsp. ginger, minced	1/2	cup water
2	Tbsp. oil	2	tsp. shoyu
1/2	cup cornstarch	1	cup sugar
4	cups oil for deep-fat frying	1/4	cup orange marmalade
2	Tbsp. oil	1-1/2	tsp. minced ginger
1/2	cup red and yellow bell	1	tsp. garlic, minced
	pepper, diced	1/4	tsp. hot pepper sauce
2	Tbsp. onion, diced	2	Tbsp. pineapple juice
Sweet and Sour Sauce		1/2	cup canned pineapple,
strips of green onion, for garnish			chopped
toasted sesame seeds, for garnish		4	Tbsp. cornstarch mixed with
			3 Tbsp. water, for thickening

CUT pork into bite-sized pieces and marinate for 30 minutes in mixture of shoyu, vermouth, garlic, ginger, and 2 tablespoons oil. Set aside. Meanwhile, make the Sweet and Sour Sauce:

In a medium saucepan combine all sweet and sour sauce ingredients except cornstarch mixture, blend well, and bring to a boil. Add cornstarch mixture. Reduce heat and simmer, stirring frequently, until thickened. Be sure and bring your sauce to a boil before adding the cornstarch, otherwise the sauce may retain an unpleasant starchy taste. (The amount of cornstarch in my recipes is just a suggestion; you may want to add more for a thicker sauce. But be careful. A little cornstarch goes a long way.)

Remove pork pieces from marinade and roll in cornstarch to coat well. Deep fry in 330 to 350-degree oil until golden brown and crispy.

In a large sauté pan, heat 2 tablespoons oil on medium-high heat. Stir-fry red and yellow bell peppers and diced onion for 2 minutes, then add *Sweet and Sour Sauce* and fold in fried pork. Let simmer 2 minutes, arrange on serving platter and garnish with long strips of green onion and toasted sesame seeds.

This is the first recipe my dad taught me to cook when I was 12 years old. Tastes great with steamed rice.

This is a real local dish with a heavy Asian influence, as well as a distinctive Hawaiian touch. Coming as I do from the hills of Wahiawa on Oahu's North Shore, I'd often drive past fields of pineapple and see all the pickers out there working, but I never gave it much thought until 1968, when I went to work for eight weeks in a Lanai pineapple field. When you see the pickers out there working it looks easy, but, man, it's really hard work.

PORK TOFU

SERVES 4

1/2 lb. lean pork, sliced thin
1-1/2 Tbsp. oil for frying
1/3 cup shoyu
2-1/2 Tbsp. sugar
1 finger fresh ginger, sliced
1 medium Maui onion, thinly sliced into half moons
1/2 bunch watercress, cut in 1-in. lengths
10 green onions, cut in 1-in. lengths
1 package firm tofu, cubed

BROWN pork in oil. Add shoyu, sugar, and ginger for that traditional flavor. Stir until sauce boils. Add onions, watercress, and green onions, reduce to medium-low heat, and let cook 2 minutes. Fold in cubed tofu and cook until tofu absorbs sauce. Pour over hot rice.

I'll never forget going as a kid to a little Japanese restaurant in a plantation town called Kahuku. It was one of those things I looked forward to on holidays. My mother would take us to that little hole in the wall where Pork Tofu was one of my favorites. That traditional flavor is what makes this recipe tick. There's no need to innovate. Something that good is just plain good. You can't improve on it.

LOCAL STYLE VEAL OSSO BUCCO WITH SHIITAKE MUSHROOMS

SERVES 4

4 veal shanks, about 1-1/2-in. thick
salt and pepper to taste
1/2 cup flour for dusting meat
3 Tbsp. oil
4 cloves garlic, crushed
1/4 cup carrots, coarsely chopped
1/2 cup onions, coarsely chopped
3 Tbsp. Chinese parsley
1 Tbsp. Five Star Spice
1/2 cup shoyu
enough chicken broth or stock to cover meat
1 cup sugar
1/2 cup sherry

SAUCE:

3 Tbsp. oil
1/2 cup sweet red and yellow bell peppers, julienned
1/2 cup onions, julienned
1/4-1/2 lb. snow peas
1 cup shiitake mushrooms, sliced
3 cups strained stock from braised veal
4 Tbsp. cornstarch mixed with 3 Tbsp. water

SPRINKLE veal shanks with salt and pepper, dust with flour, then brown in 3 tablespoons oil in large braising pan for 1 or 2 minutes per side. Add garlic, carrots, onion, Chinese parsley, Five Star Spice, and *shoyu*. Brown it all together for another 5 minutes. Cover with chicken broth or stock. Bring to a boil and add sugar and sherry. Cover with foil or oven-proof lid and braise in 350-degree oven for 1 hour, or until tender.

To make sauce, heat oil on medium-high heat in large sauté pan or wok and stir-fry vegetables 2 to 3 minutes. Add strained stock from braised veal, bring to a boil and thicken with cornstarch mixture.

It's natural when you hear the phrase "osso bucco" to automatically think Italian, but what we're doing here is taking the osso bucco cut of veal and poaching it Oriental style, then adding shiitake mushrooms. This recipe blends a great cut of meat with Oriental flavors without losing the delicate tastes of the veal or mushrooms.

TRADITIONAL BACKYARD BEEF TERIYAKI

SERVES 4 TO 6

One of the real nice things about living in Hawai'i is being able to barbecue all year long. When anybody in the neighborhood puts something on the grill, that aroma makes your taste buds go wildly out of control and you know that first chance you get you gotta make barbecue yourself. Teriyaki is one of those things everybody does, but it's a real winner. You can't go wrong with it.

2 lbs. thinly sliced steak of your choice

MARINADE:

3 cups shoyu

2 cups sugar

1/2 cup ginger, minced

4 cloves garlic, minced

4 Tbsp. green onions, thinly sliced

1/4 tsp. white pepper

2 Tbsp. Chinese parsley

2 tsp. sesame oil

BLEND marinade ingredients well, and marinate meat 4 to 6 hours in fridge.

Grill over hot coals (a hibachi seems to make the best flavor) for 2 or 3 minutes on each side, or to desired doneness. The meat is thin, so you don't want to overcook it. After it's done, try drizzling on a little of my *Special Teriyaki Glaze.*

SPECIAL TERIYAKI GLAZE:

1/2 cup shoyu

1/4 cup mirin

1/4 cup water

2 Tbsp. brown sugar

1 tsp. garlic, minced

1 tsp. ginger, minced

1 Tbsp. cornstarch mixed with 2 Tbsp. water

In a small saucepan bring all ingredients, except cornstarch mixture, to a boil. Blend cornstarch and water to make a smooth paste. Stir into pan. Reduce heat and simmer, stirring frequently, until thickened.

The Hibachi

One day when I was about eight or nine years old, my dad took the whole family out to Haleiwa Beach Park. He packed all of us and all the picnic supplies into the car and we set off for Haleiwa. After we got there and started unloading the car, he realized he had forgotten the hibachi. He immediately went scavanging around the park and somehow came up with this metal grate, possibly from an old refrigerator. He cleaned it up, put charcoal between the high roots of a banyan tree, built a fire, and set the wire grill on the roots, leveling it off with sticks. Once he got the grill going he began cooking the teriyaki meat he had marinated the night before, right there between the roots. We got out the potato salad, rice, tossed salad, kimchee and other goodies, and, within 25 minutes, we had our picnic. Believe me, it doesn't get any better than that.

I don't know why that memory has stuck in my mind all these years, but those are the kind of things no one can take away from me. Unfortunately, that's exactly the kind of experience that today's generation of youngsters are missing out on.

Some members of the older generation try to reach out to the young people to tell them about how life used to be, but often the kids aren't interested. On the other hand, I believe it's important for us to show our children what we're talking about. Even today, we can still do it—we can still capture that feeling—we just have to make the time to do it.

It's like a person who always says, "Oh, I can't go golfing with you guys because I'm too busy." We have to realize that we must make the time to enjoy life, our friends, our families. No matter what, the work will always be there. We create the situations we find ourselves in.

I believe it's important to take time to just reminisce a little, to think back to the who's, what's, when's, where's and why's of things that are important to our lives. I know I'm definitely going to take my kids back to Haleiwa Beach Park to have a barbecue—and I'll try not to forget the hibachi.

HAWAIIAN PULEHU TRI-TIP STEAK

SERVES 4 TO 6

2-1/2 lbs. tri-tip steak
     (triangular tip of the sirloin)
1/2   cup sea salt
1   Tbsp. garlic, minced
1/2   Tbsp. cracked peppercorns
1   Tbsp. sugar

LIGHT your charcoal. Rub salt, garlic, pepper, and sugar into the meat and let sit 30 minutes. Pulehu in Hawaiian means "to broil on hot embers" and that's what you do, turning the meat every 4 minutes. Total cooking time is about 10 to 15 minutes, depending upon the thickness of the cut.

It's great for tailgate or beach parties, because it's so simple and good.

This is a big piece of beef, and what makes it really good is that it's crusty on the outside and nice and rare on the inside, almost like beef sashimi. It's great eating when it's hot, and it makes the best cold sandwiches the next day after the flavors have had a chance to be absorbed all through the meat.

PULEHU RIB EYE

SERVES 4 TO 8

4   rib eye steaks (8 oz. each)
1   medium onion
enough flour to dust onion
     slices
enough oil for deep-frying
     onion slices
Special Teriyaki Glaze
     **(See Traditional Backyard
     Beef Teriyaki recipe)**

MARINADE:

2   cloves garlic, minced
1-1/2 cups shoyu
1   cup sugar
4   Tbsp. ginger, minced
2   Tbsp. green onions,
     thinly sliced
1/8 tsp. white pepper

COMBINE marinade ingredients, blend well, and marinate steak overnight in the refrigerator. Grill over charcoal or broil in the oven just the way you like it. Drizzle with *Special Teriyaki Glaze* and top with thin and crispy fried onions.

To make the fried-onion garnish, slice an onion into paper-thin circular slices, then dust slices with flour. Heat oil to 350 degrees for deep-fat frying. Drop in onions and fry until golden brown, while moving around with tongs so slices don't stick together.

This is one of my favorite cuts of beef—with its small tender strap on top, just the right amount of fat for flavor and tenderness, and then that tasty eye. I like to eat it "blue," cooked just on the outside and still raw inside. Mmmmmm!

STIR-FRIED BEEF WITH HONAUNAU SNOW PEAS

SERVES 4

1   lb. lean beef
2   tsp. cornstarch
1   tsp. sugar
1   Tbsp. shoyu
1-1/2 Tbsp. sweet vermouth
1-1/2 Tbsp. water
3   Tbsp. oil
1/2 finger of fresh ginger, sliced
1/2 lb. snow peas
1   cup chicken broth
salt and pepper to taste

THICKENING AGENT:

a well-blended mixture of
1   tsp. sugar
1   Tbsp. cornstarch
1   Tbsp. water

SLICE beef thinly, against grain. Combine cornstarch, sugar, shoyu and vermouth, and massage into meat for 2 or 3 minutes. Let sit 2 or 3 minutes to marinate. Heat 1 tablespoon oil on medium-high heat in wok or sauté pan. Stir-fry ginger a minute or 2. Add snow peas and stir-fry 1 or 2 minutes more. Remove and set aside.

Add another 2 tablespoons of oil and stir-fry beef on medium-high heat until beef begins to brown, then add broth, peas, and ginger and bring to a boil. Season with salt and pepper to taste. Add thickening agent, return to a boil, and stir until thickened. Serve with hot rice.

This is a real simple dish. The hardest part is cutting the beef and cleaning the snow peas. The cooking goes real quick. Before you know it, you're sitting down enjoying delicious tender morsels of beef and sweet snow peas from Honaunau. I can see you now, licking your chops. Remember, don't overcook the snow peas.

HULI HULI (ROTISSERIE) BEEF

SERVES 10 TO 16

1   **whole cross-rib roast (4 lbs.), or bottom round, or tri-tip**

4   **cups sweet vermouth, for basting**

MARINADE:

1   **Tbsp. cracked peppercorns sea salt, as needed, up to 1 cup**

2   **Tbsp. garlic, minced**

2   **Tbsp. ginger, minced**

COMBINE marinade ingredients, massage into roast, and let marinate 15 minutes. Place roast on skewer and secure into rotisserie over hot coals. (Don't cover.)

Plan on about 2 hours cooking time. Baste every 10 to 20 minutes with sweet vermouth, until the last 30 minutes. Then baste about every 5 minutes. If you don't have a rotisserie, it can be done in a closed outdoor barbecue system by turning the meat every half hour and basting in the same manner as for the rotisserie method.

It's very impressive when you go to a backyard party or a family gathering and see this massive side of beef turning over the coals, and you ask yourself how you can do it at home. That's why I've included this recipe, so you can do rotisserie beef yourself and have it look awesome and impressive, as well as have it taste real good.

Sam Choy's: The Restaurant

My family, especially my sister Wai Sun, has always been involved in my restaurants. In July 1991, we opened Sam's Diner—just a simple, walk-up type of deal—at the bowling alley in Kona. It was a typically low-key venture. To publicize the operation, I would get off from work at the Kona Hilton, change clothes, and walk over to the bowling alley. My sister and I would prepare a couple of plates of food, walk up and down the aisles, find a place to sit down, and eat. People would recognize me and say, "Eh, Sam, what you doing here?" "Oh, we just took over the diner," I'd tell them. I did that every night for a week, because different leagues bowled on different nights. After the first night, business doubled, and so on, and it's been busy ever since.

Earlier, we had been approached by an investor to lease the space where our restaurant now stands. We had a lot of unanswered questions about the deal, and we really didn't have much money at the time. A year or two went by before we decided to go for it. It was a gamble, opening up in this industrial area—I know the bank certainly felt it was a gamble. It was really scary when we opened in November 1991.

Again, we decided not to mount much of an advertising campaign. We were concerned that if we opened and a lot of peple came storming through, we wouldn't be able to handle it, so we opted for a real "soft" opening.

Well, the first day came, and we had about 20 workers standing by. We must have looked really greedy . . . and foolish. All of us were waiting and waiting, and only five or ten people came in the whole day. I can laugh about it now, but it certainly wasn't funny at the time.

"What are we going to do?" we thought. A few of the workers volunteered to put flyers on car windshields to let people know about the restaurant. From about the third or fourth day, it slowly started getting busier. It wasn't magic. The first two or three months were still slow, but every day was a little busier than the one before.

The whole business was built up by word-of-mouth. We knew, of course, that word-of-mouth publicity could work both ways. One person would come in, have a great time, and might tell 10 others. Another person would come in, have a bad experience, and would surely tell at least 100 people. That's just the way it works.

We started off really low-key—serving the food on paper plates. I had built up a following from the Kona Hilton, so when these customers came into our restaurant and got their food on paper plates, they said, "Paper plates? Wow, Sam, not for real, eh?" I tried to cover by saying, "Oh, no, our regular plates haven't come in yet." We quickly decided that we had to offer table service and have waitresses.

We shipped over a 50-place setting of brown plates, butter plates, soup cups, and coffee mugs from Laie that Wai Sun had bought nearly 10 years earlier, when we opened the original Sam's Place in 1980. Over the years, whenever she came across sales on pots, pans or kitchen equipment, she would buy and store them in Laie, a little at a time. When we opened this restaurant, we called the movers, packed everything, and shipped it all over. It saved us a lot of money. We didn't come in and just buy everything overnight. It was a long-term thing.

The restaurant is still run like a family. We have some extremely good, young employees. When we hire, we're not necessarily looking at a person's academic qualifications, but more for one's character and heart. We can teach them what they need to learn. Some of our employees started out working at the bowling alley. If they showed an interest in either the cooking or the business side of food service, then we offered them an opportunity to pursue a career with us. We're very proud to see how far some of them have come.

The crew at the restaurant works under a lot of pressure. It's not easy running a restaurant, and we set high standards for everyone. I try to help the young staff and always try to stay very positive when working with them. I believe it's important for them to feel that they can accomplish anything they want in life by taking one step at a time, staying positive, and working hard.

I find there are aspects to running a restaurant that are similar to coaching a football team. I often think about all of the people who have touched my life, especially my coaches when I played sports out at Kahuku, people like Famika Anae, Harry Kaahanui, Gilbert Hatter, Tommy Heffernan and Clarence Mills, as well as some of the teachers, like Charles Bernaba. I can still hear Harry Kaahanui telling me, "Sam, you can be anything you want in life. Whatever you do, give it a hundred percent."

Famika Anae, who had a real rah-rah coaching style, would say, "Okay, men, let's play as a team. Think positive; no negative attitudes." We could be down 44-0 at halftime, and he'd say, "Be positive. Let's go, men. Let's go do it!" These are the things that I've carried throughout my life. In my own way, I try to impart that kind of encouragement to our young staff.

The kitchen at Sam Choy's is designed so it is visible to the customers. Besides giving our customers something to see while their order is being prepared, this feature affects the way our cooks and kitchen workers conduct themselves. First of all, they always have to be extremely conscious about cleanliness, which is very important to me. Secondly, because people are watching, it keeps the employees focused and always aware that they must conduct themselves in a professional manner. This, I believe, adds to their self-esteem.

So here we are today, in an industrial-style building in the middle of an industrial park. We're proud of the fact that, on any given day, you might find construction workers dining alongside lawyers, and maybe even a celebrity or two. They're all here, sitting at tables, getting fed. And what are they eating? Sam Choy's local grinds, featuring old-time flavors from way back when.

This multicultural mix, this laid back ambiance, is not lost on tourists. You'd be amazed to see how many tourists find their way to our restaurant. They ask me, "Do you cook like this for us and another way for the locals?" "No," I tell them. "I cook this way all the time." You should see their faces light up. Travelers today are smart; they're looking for something that's true to the place that they visit.

If what I do moves them, these visitors go home and tell their friends and neighbors, "When you go to Kona, Hawaii, you've got to eat at Sam Choy's Restaurant." Now, after three-and-a half years in business, we're getting the friends of the friends of the friends who first came in and "discovered" us. The networking grows, and now people write in a visit to Sam Choy's restaurant on their travel calendars. They always say they enjoy the great service, great food, great value, and the overall experience of the restaurant itself— it's the real thing.

People look at us now and they think, "Hey, look how busy the restaurant is. They must be making tons of money." Well, with the high cost of running a restaurant, that's not the case, and that's not how I measure success, anyway. Then there are those who say, "Oh, who's this guy, Sam Choy? Where's he been all these years?" Well, let me tell you, like so many other "overnight" successes, he's been struggling for a long time.

PAPA CHOY'S BEEF TOMATO

SERVES 6

When I used to come home from school as a kid, my dad would go to the refrigerator and bring out all these vegetables and wash and chop and slice them and lay them out in a pan, then take some beef and slice it thin and marinate it, then stir-fry it all together and within minutes I'd be sitting there eating it. It's just amazing how quick he could do it, and how good it tasted.

1 lb.	round steak, or flank steak, or beef of your choice
1	Tbsp. oil
3	medium fresh tomatoes, cut into wedges
1	medium onion, sliced into half moons
1	large green pepper, sliced into strips
4	stalks green onions, cut into 1-in. lengths
2	stalks celery, thinly sliced on the diagonal
salt and pepper to taste	

MARINADE:

1	Tbsp. shoyu
1	Tbsp. sherry
1	Tbsp. oil
1-1/2	tsp. sugar
1	clove garlic, minced
1/4	finger fresh ginger, sliced

SAUCE:

1	cup chicken broth
1	Tbsp. cornstarch
2	Tbsp. shoyu
2	tsp. salt
2	tsp. brown sugar
1	tsp. oyster sauce

SLICE beef thinly into strips, or bite-sized pieces. Combine marinade ingredients, mix well and massage into meat. Let marinate for 30 minutes. Combine sauce ingredients, mix well, and set aside.

Heat 1 tablespoon oil in a wok or frying pan on medium-high. Stir-fry beef about 2 minutes, remove beef from pan and set aside. Add vegetables to pan and stir-fry until onions are translucent, about 3 minutes. Add sauce to vegetables. Cook about 2 minutes, until it comes to a boil. Add beef and adjust seasonings with salt and pepper. Serve over hot rice.

My dad taught me this one when I was about 14.

BIG ISLAND BEEF SHORTRIBS

SERVES 4

This recipe is real easy and really **LIGHT** your charcoal. While it's good.

2	lbs. beef shortribs, 3/8-in. thick
1	Tbsp. sea salt, rock salt, or Kosher salt
1	tsp. cracked peppercorns
1	tsp. garlic, minced
1	cup vermouth
1	Tbsp. *shoyu*

getting hot, mix salt and pepper and rub into meat. Massage in the garlic, then pour vermouth over ribs and drizzle with the shoyu. Let marinate 20 to 30 minutes, then grill to perfection.

Cowboys or paniolo are always having big outdoor cookouts, and shortribs is one of their favorites for barbecuing. Asian groups use it too, but I like the Hawaiian way: rub in the seasoned salt and let it sit a few minutes, then throw it on the coals. It doesn't get any better.

BRAISED ANISE BEEF BRISKET

SERVES 6 TO 8

3	Tbsp. shoyu
1	tsp. ginger, minced
1	tsp. garlic, minced
3	lbs. beef brisket
3	Tbsp. oil
1	qt. chicken broth (or enough to cover meat)
2	Tbsp. anise seeds (whole)
1	finger fresh ginger root, crushed
4	cloves garlic, crushed
1-1/2 cups sugar	

RUB shoyu, minced ginger, and minced garlic into meat, then brown in oil. Cover with chicken broth. Add anise seeds, crushed ginger, crushed garlic, and sugar. Bring to a boil, then reduce heat and let simmer, covered, for 1-1/2 hours, or until tender. Set aside until cooled slightly. Slice thin and serve with steamed rice. It's good cold, too.

This is a real easy one, and it's different.

This dish is good either hot or cold. It tastes a little like licorice, but it's not as sweet. It has a real nice flavor, a different sort of taste.

The Art of Cooking

My mother always loved art—she loved to paint with oils—and that really inspired me to think artistically, to prepare food creatively and attractively. The thought may not be original to me, but I've always felt that cooking is like art. Rather than merely making your dish look attractive—like an artist, your mind, your heart, and your feelings come out through your hands when you cook.

A painter sees a subject through his eyes and remembers it in his mind. Through his imagination, he creates something new, expressing it through his heart onto the canvas, just as a writer expresses his feelings through his heart onto paper.

If an artist wanted to, he could always take a simple snapshot of something, blow it up, and say, "Voila, there it is." Instead, the artist interprets his subject, labors over it, and puts a part of himself into his art. It's the same with cooking.

Let's say you put 10 people in a room and told them, "Today, we're all going to cook chili. We're going to provide you with the basic recipe and the ingredients." You could then bring in a panel of judges to taste the chili. I'd guarantee you that each person's chili would taste different, some better than others. The reason is simple: some members of the group did it because they were told to do it, while others did it because they enjoyed doing it . . . and the difference will always show.

When I cook, the process is like an artist visualizing what he wants to put on his canvas. Let's say I have a wonderful piece of fresh fish. I automatically visualize the entire process in my mind. I think, "How do I present it? What goes good with it?"

Like an artist, a chef needs the freedom to take his subject to the edge, while maintaining a proper balance—you wouldn't put chocolate sauce on steamed fish, for example. I might think, "Ahh, it's such a fresh fish, I don't want to smother it with sauce. Maybe a light butter sauce, with just a hint of shoyu to be different. Okay, I'll saute it lightly with just a little butter and shoyu sauce. What kind of vegetables? Steamed won bok or steamed kai choy. Yes, that's it."

My mind is racing all the time. If I see a fresh piece of mahimahi or opakapaka, my mind might say, "Ginger pesto," or, "Shiitake butter cream sauce. Yes, and serve it with plain steamed rice. You can't beat that."

I put my heart into what I do. I imagine someone taking a first bite, a smile growing from ear to ear, and eyes lighting up. To see that is worth more to me than all the money in the world, because you know you've touched somebody. You know you've touched them in their heart, and they'll never forget it.

I'm honored and humbled when people come up to me and say, "Sam, you're a magician," or, "Sam, you're different." There are a lot of great chefs in Hawai'i. I think if something comes through that maybe makes me a little different, it is my love for what I do. I enjoy talking to people. I enjoy the simple things in life—like the natural beauty, the mana of these islands. I enjoy all of it.

I hope that everyone who cooks can come to see themselves as artists, visualizing the raw canvas, allowing their imaginations free rein, and putting their hearts into it. As a matter of fact, shouldn't it be that way with everything you do in life?

POULTRY

CHICKEN TOFU
WITH WATERCRESS

SERVES 4 TO 6

This is very simple to make. Just be sure to wait until the end to fold in the tofu—you don't want to overcook it and have it crumble away to mush. And remember to use firm tofu.

12	boneless chicken thighs, cut into 1-in. cubes
2	Tbsp. oil
2	medium onions, sliced into half moons
1	bunch watercress, cut into 1-in. sections
1	block firm tofu, cubed

salt and pepper to taste

MARINADE:

2	Tbsp. shoyu
1/2	tsp. garlic, minced
1/2	tsp. brown sugar
1	Tbsp. salad oil

SAUCE:

1/2	cup shoyu
2	Tbsp. mirin
1	Tbsp. garlic, minced
1	Tbsp. ginger, minced
1/2	tsp. salt
1/4	tsp. white pepper
1-1/2 tsp. brown sugar	

MIX marinade ingredients together well and marinate chicken for 30 minutes.

In a medium saucepan, fry chicken in 2 tablespoons oil on medium-high heat until it is semi-brown. Add sauce ingredients and bring to a boil. Add onions and watercress and cook 2 to 3 minutes. Add tofu, reduce heat and simmer for about 3 minutes, until tofu absorbs some of the liquid. Adjust seasoning with salt and pepper.

This makes a great meal served straight from the skillet with hot steamed rice.

Hibiscus Salad?

When I got my first paying job at the Hyatt Kuilima Resort, now called the Turtle Bay Hilton & Country Club., I remember how excited I was—like it was the best thing that had ever happened to me. After all, I was getting paid for something I loved to do.

I was determined to be the best worker I could be, so one of the things I did was refine my knife skills to a science. I would go into our yard and trim all my mom's hedges and flowers. It drove her crazy. Then I'd go out back, take an old cutting board, and just chop away. I really got carried away, because I wanted to make sure that my knife skills were good. After all, that's where it all starts—cutting everything uniformly, balancing, blending and contrasting colors. I didn't cook and eat the shrubbery, of course, I was just fascinated by the different angles and cuts.

Although that job was my first big opportunity, it also presented me with my first setback. I had been hired as a cook's helper, but all they had me doing was washing pots and pans. At first I was disappointed, naturally, but then I told myself, "Well, maybe I can learn something about this business from another angle," and it turned out great. As the chefs brought their pots and pans to me to wash, I got to taste all of the different sauces. Ha! I was very fortunate, because I learned so much and educated my taste buds very quickly.

I believe you can learn something new every day, no matter where you are or what you're doing. That's why I know I haven't achieved my best work yet. I'm just starting to get better.

MACADAMIA NUT CHICKEN BREAST

SERVES 4

4   chicken breasts
        (6 to 8 oz. each)
1-1/2 cups panko or bread crumbs
1   cup macadamia nuts,
        chopped
2   Tbsp. parsley, chopped
1-1/2 cups flour
3   whole eggs, whipped
1/2   cup oil

MARINADE:

1   cup shoyu
4   Tbsp. brown sugar
1   Tbsp. ginger, minced
1   Tbsp. garlic, minced
1/2   cup sherry

PINEAPPLE/PAPAYA MARMALADE:

1/2   cup papaya, diced
1/2   cup pineapple, diced
3   Tbsp. sugar
fresh mint or spearmint

COMBINE marinade ingredients and marinate chicken for 30 to 45 minutes.

Mix panko, macadamia nuts, and parsley. Remove chicken from marinade and blot off excess liquid. Dust chicken with flour, dip into eggs, then into panko/macadamia nut mixture. Press breading firmly onto chicken.

Coat pan with enough oil to cover bottom. (Don't use all of the 1/2 cup at once. Chicken will absorb it as it cooks and you may need to add more as you go.) Heat oil on medium-high and sauté chicken 3 to 4 minutes on each side until golden brown. Don't overcook. Serve with *Pineapple/Papaya Marmalade* as a dipping sauce.

To make marmalade, combine papaya, pineapple, and sugar. Simmer in a heavy saucepan for 20 minutes, stirring occasionally. Try adding some fresh chopped mint or spearmint to the marmalade; it's really, really good.

It's great to be living in Kona, where macadamia nuts are so plentiful, and it's exciting to utilize them as one of Hawai'i's best kept cooking secrets. We often look at mac nuts as just something tourists buy, or something for a dessert or snack, but they add a very unique taste when used as part of the entrée. The mac nut crust in this recipe ensures that the chicken will be moist inside, while nice and crunchy and nutty on the outside.

ROTISSERIE CHICKEN

SERVES 4 TO 6

In Hawaiian, huli means to turn, and huli huli means to turn over and over, and that's just what you do in cooking this island favorite.

2	fryers (2 to 3 lb. each)
4	Tbsp. salad oil
1	Tbsp. garlic, minced
1	Tbsp. salt
1/2	tsp. paprika
1	tsp. coriander seeds, crushed
1/2	tsp. black pepper

SPLIT each chicken down the backbone, but leave attached at breast. Remove neck bone. Rub chickens with oil and garlic and let sit for 30 minutes. Mix remaining ingredients and sprinkle on chickens so that they are seasoned very well. Secure on rotisserie and roast 45 minutes to 1 hour. Basting is not necessary.

If you don't have a rotisserie, you can grill on a hibachi for the same amount of time, turning every 10 to 15 minutes, or broil in your oven, 45 minutes to 1 hour, turning with the same frequency.

If you don't feel like turning it, you can bake it in your oven at 350 degrees, breast side up.

At every fair and big event in Hawai'i, you'll see huli huli chickens turning, dozens at a time, on rotisseries over hot coals. It smells so good and tastes so good and is so easy to do. You don't need a rotisserie, just keep turning it over hot charcoal. Use mesquite. Chicken doesn't get much easier, or more delicious.

SAM'S SPECIAL "BIG-O" THANKSGIVING TURKEY

SERVES 6 TO 8

For as long as I can remember, after every Thanksgiving dinner two things happened— one, I'd feel like I ate myself into outer space and, two, I'd feel like I needed to take about a year off from eating. So that's one of the reasons I came up with the "Big O" (meaning zero fat) turkey dinner. With this meal you feel full, yet by the next day you feel like you're ready to get right back into your normal eating schedule.

2-3	lbs. boneless, skinless turkey breast
1	tsp. salt
1/4	tsp. white pepper
2	cups chicken broth
1/2	cup carrots, chopped
1/2	cup celery, chopped
1/2	cup onions, chopped
2	Tbsp. cornstarch mixed with 2 Tbsp. water

RUB salt and pepper into turkey breast for 2 to 3 minutes.

Pour 1 cup of chicken broth into bottom of roasting pan. Add vegetables. Place turkey in pan and cover tightly with foil, or oven-proof lid.

Roast in 375-degree oven for 30 minutes, then reduce to 350 and cook 20 minutes more. Remove foil and brown for about 10 minutes. Total cooking time should be about 1 hour. Remove from oven and cool before slicing.

Place drippings and cooked vegetables in saucepan. Add 1 cup chicken broth and bring to a boil. Add cornstarch mixture to boiling water and simmer 2 to 3 minutes. Strain and set aside.

Slice turkey breast and serve with no-fat mashed potatoes, no-fat stuffing, and no-fat cranberry sauce (recipes follow).

I like to boil the potatoes with garlic and chives, which adds a lot of flavor, and use chicken broth in place of butter and milk.

STUFFING:

1	tsp. poultry seasoning
1	cup apples, chopped
1	cup onion, chopped
1	cup celery, chopped
2	cups chicken broth
3	cups toasted croutons (or more, for dryer stuffing)

salt and pepper to taste

Combine all ingredients except croutons. Bring to a boil and simmer until vegetables are soft, then fold in croutons.

CRANBERRY SAUCE:

1	cup fresh pineapple juice
1	cup fresh orange juice
3	cups whole cranberries
1	whole orange, sliced, with rind

Bring all ingredients to a boil, then cook down to the consistency of jam, 25 to 30 minutes, or until reduced to the desired consistency. It tastes good as is but, if you want it sweeter, add a little sugar.

SAM CHOY'S AWARD-WINNING ROAST DUCK

SERVES 4 TO 6

Roasting duck the traditional Chinese way is a lot of work, but I've found an easy way to do it that I think tastes just as good.

2   ducks, 3 to 4 lbs. each
3/4   cup shoyu

DRY MARINADE:

1   Tbsp. salt
1   Tbsp. garlic salt
1   tsp. garlic powder
1   tsp. paprika
1/2   tsp. white pepper
1   Tbsp. coriander seeds
       (whole)

REMOVE wing tips, neck flap, tail end, excess fat, and drumstick knuckles. Rinse both ducks. Place in a dish, and pour shoyu over them. Roll the ducks in the shoyu and let sit for about 10 minutes. Keep rolling in the shoyu every 3 to 4 minutes.

Preheat oven to 550 degrees. Mix all dry marinade ingredients. Place ducks breast side up on roasting rack in a roasting pan and sprinkle thoroughly with marinade. Put a little marinade inside cavities.

Roast in 550-degree oven for 30 minutes. Reduce heat to 325. Cook for 1 hour, or until meat thermometer registers an internal temperature of 170 to 175 degrees. No basting is necessary.

Serve with steamed rice.

Everybody likes this one. Lots of people rave about it. It's like a shining star in our menu. The best award we've ever won is the people's award, and this dish keeps winning it over and over again.

SWEET-AND-SOUR CHICKEN BREASTS WITH TROPICAL FRUITS

SERVES 4

4   chicken breasts (6 to 8 oz. each)

1-1/2 cups flour

3   Tbsp. oil

1   cup fresh pineapple, diced

1   cup fresh papaya, chopped

1   cup mangoes, or tropical fruit of your choice, chopped

MARINADE:

1/2   cup shoyu

1/2   cup oil

2   Tbsp. mirin

1   Tbsp. garlic, minced

1   Tbsp. ginger, minced

1/2   tsp. salt

1/4   tsp. white pepper

2   Tbsp. cornstarch

1-1/2 tsp. brown sugar

SWEET-AND-SOUR SAUCE:

1/2   cup tomato catsup

1/2   cup vinegar

1/2   cup water

2   tsp. shoyu

1   cup sugar

1/4   cup orange marmalade

1-1/2 tsp. ginger, minced

1   tsp. garlic, minced

1/4   tsp. hot pepper sauce

2   Tbsp. pineapple juice

2   Tbsp. cornstarch blended with 1-1/2 Tbsp. water

GARNISH:

green onion strips

sprigs of fresh Chinese parsley

COMBINE marinade ingredients and marinate chicken for 30 minutes.

Make sweet-and-sour sauce by combining all ingredients, except cornstarch mixture, in a medium saucepan. Bring to a boil. Add cornstarch mixture, reduce heat and simmer, stirring frequently, until thickened.

Blot excess liquid off chicken and dust with flour to coat. Pan fry in 3 tablespoons oil until golden brown, about 4 minutes per side on medium heat. Remove chicken, set aside, and keep warm.

Discard excess oil in pan, leaving about 1 tablespoon. Stir-fry fruit in oil for 2 minutes. Add sweet-and-sour sauce and heat through.

Arrange chicken breasts on serving platter, pour sauce over chicken and garnish with green onions and Chinese parsley.

I really like doing this dish because it gives you a whole new twist on cooking, beyond the basic sweet and sour sauce. Adding the fresh tropical fruits really makes it good, and different. It takes away the boredom.

CHICKEN HEKKA

SERVES 4 TO 6

I like to eat this on a Sunday afternoon after a heavy week-end of parties. It's kind of light, with vegetables and noodles, and helps me ease down on my eating. It's real easy because you make it in one pot, and it doesn't take long to put together.

2-1/2 lbs. boneless chicken thighs
   or breasts
3   Tbsp. oil
1/2 finger crushed ginger
1   No. 2 can sliced bamboo
   shoots
10 stalks green onions,
   cut in 1-in. lengths
1   round onion,
   cut in half moon slices
1   medium carrot, julienned
1   lb. shiitake mushrooms,
   sliced
2   stalks celery, julienned
1/2 lb. watercress,
   cut into 1-in. lengths
1   bundle (2 oz.) bean threads,
   cooked and cut into
   1-in. lengths

MARINADE:
1/2 cup shoyu
1/2 cup oil
2   Tbsp. mirin
1   Tbsp. garlic, minced
1   Tbsp. ginger, minced
1/2 tsp. salt
1/4 tsp. white pepper
2   Tbsp. cornstarch
1-1/2 tsp. brown sugar

SAKE SAUCE:
1/2 cup sugar
3/4 cup shoyu
1/2 cup chicken broth
1/2 cup sake

COMBINE marinade ingredients and marinate chicken for 30 minutes.

Slice vegetables, mix, and set aside. Blend *Sake Sauce* ingredients and set aside.

Brown chicken in 3 tablespoons oil to which you have added a half finger of crushed ginger. Add all vegetables and cook for 1 minute. Add *Sake Sauce* and bean threads and simmer on medium for 5 minutes.

Serve with hot steamed rice.

HERB/GARLIC ROTISSERIE CORNISH GAME HENS

SERVES 6

When I was growing up I called Cornish game hens "baby chickens," because that's what they looked like. I like cooking this because it's easy and it's something you can prepare ahead of time, throw on the rotisserie just before the guests arrive, and an hour later have a great meal. It also looks special, like you went to a lot of trouble.

6	Cornish game hens
3/4	cups softened butter
2	Tbsp. garlic, minced
	Juice from 2 tangerines, or from 1 large orange
1	tsp. fresh mint, minced
1	tsp. green onion, minced
1	tsp. fresh Chinese parsley, minced
3	Tbsp. shoyu
1	Tbsp. sea salt

PREPARE rotisserie and light coals.

Rinse game hens and pat dry. In mixing bowl, blend all ingredients (except hens) into a paste. Rub herb paste thoroughly over the game hens and into the cavities, as well.

Secure onto the rotisserie and roast for 55 minutes to 1 hour, until golden brown. If you don't have a rotisserie, you can bake the game hens in a 350-degree oven for the same amount of time, until brown.

EASY CHICKEN LAU LAU

SERVES 4

This is a traditional Hawaiian dish that goes back thousands of years. You cook it in a steamer basket instead of an underground oven, though. It's not hard to do and is very good and good for you—real moist and flavorful, with healthy ingredients.

4   boneless chicken breasts
2   oz. salted butterfish
1   Tbsp. Hawaiian salt
20   luau (taro) leaves
     (or fresh spinach leaves)
8   ti leaves for wrappers
     (or corn husks, or tin foil)
enough string to tie wrappers
     around lau lau

LEAVE chicken breasts whole. It tastes better to leave the skin on, but you can remove it if you'd like. Sprinkle chicken with salt. Cut fish into four equal pieces.

Rinse luau leaves, trim stems, remove larger veins. Remove part of back rib of each ti leaf so the leaves become pliable (or cook ti leaves in microwave on high for a minute or so, to make them flexible). (Ti leaves may be obtained from a florist if you don't have any growing in your yard.) Divide luau leaves into four piles of five each, with the largest leaf on the bottom of the pile. If you are using spinach in place of luau leaves, it won't be as flavorful, but it will still be good. You may have to use more spinach leaves because they're smaller.

Place a chicken breast and a piece of butterfish on each pile of leaves and sprinkle with a little salt, if desired. Gathering up the luau leaves around the chicken and fish, wrap into a tight bundle and place bundle in the middle of 2 ti leaves you have laid over each other in the form of a cross. The bundle should be placed directly in the center of the cross. Gather up the ti leaves and tie tightly with string just above bundle to make a purse, securing the lau lau inside.

Place in steamer and steam for 1 hour and 45 minutes. Check occasionally to make sure there's enough water in the steamer.

To serve, remove lau lau from ti leaves and discard ti leaves.

• HIBACHI CHICKEN BREAST

SERVES 3 TO 6

Hibachi chicken is a great potluck dish. You can have it already marinated and bring it in a ziplock in the cooler, with the hibachi in the trunk. When you get to the potluck, you fire up the hibachi and, when the coals are ready, you throw on the chicken and in about 45 minutes you'll have something that will make everybody happy.

6   chicken breasts

MARINADE:

1   tsp. sesame oil

1-1/2 cups shoyu

2   cloves garlic, minced

1   cup sugar

1/4   cup ginger, minced

2   Tbsp. green onions, thinly sliced

1   Tbsp. Chinese parsley, minced

1/8   tsp. white pepper

PREPARE and light coals in hibachi. Blend marinade ingredients thoroughly and marinate chicken breasts for 30 minutes.

Grill over coals, turning every 2 to 3 minutes, for a total cooking time of 8 to 10 minutes. If you prefer, you may pan fry the chicken breasts, or broil them in the oven. The cooking time is the same.

It goes great with stir-fried vegetables and steamed rice, or cut julienned style into strips and tossed with mixed greens and served with one of my signature salad dressings. My favorite way is on a whole wheat bun with mayonnaise, lettuce, tomatoes, and onions. Mmmmm. I'm getting hungry!

Return to Hukilau Bay

If you drive to Laie out on the North Shore, you will see Laie Bay, nicknamed "Hukilau Bay," because a big hukilau was held there on Saturdays as part of the luau that my father catered for the church. The men, women and children from the community would join the tourists , helping to haul in the nets. The flat, sandy bottom there made it an ideal place to set out the long nets to catch the fish that came into the bay to feed.

I have many memories of the luau and the hukilau. When I was only about seven years old, one of my chores was to mix the punch—a mixture of syrup, water and pineapple juice. My father always told me that the secret to making good punch was to use lots of ice. Stirring the mixture in a big stainless steel pot with a big paddle, I remember feeling scared because I imagined if I fell in the giant vat, I would drown.

If the tourists ate a whole lot, sometimes we would run out of long rice or other foodstuffs. At such times, my father would tell us to get some bread and make sandwiches with the kalua pork. Man, the tourists loved the kalua pork sandwiches!

The men would set the nets out at about 10:30. I can still close my eyes and see it all: the morning sun behind them; one guy oaring as all the nets go peeling off the back of the boat. I remember the net being about 100-150 feet long. After they had set the net out, they would put the lau, made of *ti* leaves and rope, to scare the fish towards the net. The highest portion of the net had a pocket, so the fish would get trapped in the pocket.

Back in those days, there was always one man in charge of laying the net for the hukilau. It was a big thing to be the one in charge. The first one was Jubilee Logan, a handsome, white-haired man. He would stand out there in his malo, and, like a general, he would command, "Ready on the right! Ready on the left!" All the eyes of the people standing on each side waited for his signal. When his hand went down, everyone started to pull.

After Jubilee Logan retired, Moke Hiram took over, then, after him, George Nihipali, then Bob Kahawai and Manawela Kalili. I looked up to these gentlemen—each with his own, distinctive style and personality—as the greats of Laie.

As everybody was working the net in, the general would yell out, "Huki on the right! Huki on the left. Come on kids, pull, huki huki." The net had to be pulled in evenly, and the lau brought in evenly. Once you got the net in, you had to close the net together, pulling until you had all the fish chased into the pocket.

At that point, the excitement and drama would really build, because everybody was so eager to see what was in the net. The divers would swim out, bobbing up and down, signaling with their hands to show the size of the fish in the net and yelling, "Big fish!" As the net got closer to the shore, you could hear them calling out, "Weke ula, oio, moi, mullet, awa," and whatever else was caught. The turtles were let go, even in those days. It's amazing—that bay produced fish every Saturday for many, many years.

All the local families who turned out to help went home with fish in their pockets or under their arms, walking across the beach to the road. It was worth it for them to come out and help, and it was a nice opportunity for the tourists to mingle with the locals.

I'll never forget those magical days. Of course I understand that times have changed, but, hey, the bay is still there, the sandy beach is still there, still beautiful. The trade winds still blow, and you can still look out and gaze upon Goat Island, Little Island, Lizard Island, and Laie Point.

I take my kids there, to go swimming in the bay, and I tell them about Jubilee Logan, Moke Hiram, George Nihipali, Bob Kahawai, Manawela Kalili—and the great hukilau of Laie Bay.

FISH & SEAFOOD

WARNING
NO TRESPASSING
LOITERING
(6 PM - 6 AM)
VIOLATORS WILL BE PROSECUTED

HEALTH REGULATION
DO NOT WALK OR STAND
ON FISH DISPLAY BOARDS

BAKED WHOLE FISH IN COCONUT CREAM

SERVES 2 TO 4

Lots of people are afraid to cook fish because they hear too many horror stories about how they can mess it up. But it's not hard to do it right. The secret is to use only the freshest fish and seafood, don't over season, and don't overcook. Most people overcook fish—they don't realize how quickly it cooks—and that's why it doesn't taste good. A lot of people don't think they like fish just because they've never eaten it when it was properly cooked. Old-fashioned cookbooks say fish is done when you can flake it with a fork, but by then it's already overcooked. Fish is done the minute it loses its translucency in the middle and becomes opaque. It doesn't take long. Sometimes only a minute or two. Fish is the original fast food. If you're going to overcook it, you might as well save your money and buy a can of tuna. I think most fish tastes best when it's a little raw in the middle, but maybe that's an acquired taste. Of course, today, as more and more people discover sushi and sashimi, it is an acquired taste that is becoming more common.

Coming from Laie, a little fishing village, I remember watching the Polynesian people cook big, whole, ti leaf-wrapped fish in the imu. Those memories inspired this recipe.

1	whole fish of your choice (2 to 3 lbs.), scaled, gutted, and gilled (with head and tail attached)
1/2	tsp. salt
1	Tbsp. ginger, minced
6	cleaned ti leaves
1	cup onions, diced
1/2	tsp. white pepper
2	cups canned coconut milk, mixed with 1/2 tsp. salt

PREheat oven to 350 degrees.

Score fish diagonally both ways to make diamonds and sprinkle with salt and the ginger. Use 3 ti leaves to cover the bottom of an oven-proof baking dish large enough to hold the fish, then place fish on ti leaves. Blend onions and pepper with coconut milk/salt mixture and pour over fish. Cover with remaining 3 ti leaves. Cover baking dish with lid or foil and bake at 350 degrees for 35 to 45 minutes, depending on the size of the fish. Check at 35 minutes for doneness. Don't overcook.

• STEAMED WHOLE OPAKAPAKA

SERVES 2 TO 4

I love catching opakapaka, knowing there's a million ways to cook it. One of the most impressive is steaming it whole, then presenting it on a large platter set right on the table.

1	whole opakapaka (2 to 3 lbs.), gutted, scaled, and gilled (with head and tail attached)
1/2	cup light salad oil
1	Tbsp. shoyu

GINGER PESTO:

1/2	cup Chinese parsley, minced
1/2	cup green onions, minced
1/4	cup ginger, minced
1	tsp. Hawaiian salt
3/4	cups salad oil
1/2	tsp. white pepper

MIX all pesto ingredients until well blended and set aside. Score fish diagonally in two directions to make diamonds. Place in steamer. Pour pesto over fish. Steam 15 to 18 minutes, or until done.

Heat 1/2 cup oil until almost smoking, then pour over cooked fish; the oil should be so hot it sizzles as you pour it. Drizzle 1 tablespoon shoyu over top.

Serve with hot steamed rice and a green salad. This is my favorite. Good, good, good!

• STEAMED MAHIMAHI LAU LAU

SERVES 4

Using a steaming method is a good way to cook this moist, delicate fish. It helps retain the moisture, texture, and fresh flavor of this great-tasting, mild white fish.

2　**cups carrots, finely julienned**

2　**cups zucchini, finely julienned**

1　**cup shiitake mushrooms, sliced**

8　**ti leaves**

12　**fresh mahimahi fillets (2 oz each) (don't substitute any other fish)**

salt and pepper to taste

enough string to tie each lau lau

HERB SAUCE:

1-1/2 **cup mayonnaise**

1　**Tbsp. shoyu**

1　**Tbsp. fresh dill, chopped**

MIX carrots and zucchini together and divide into 4 equal portions. Divide mushrooms into 4 equal portions. Mix herb sauce ingredients and set aside. Remove hard rib from ti leaves to make flexible, or cook leaves on high in microwave for 1 minute to soften.

To build each lau lau, first make a ti leaf cross on the table by laying 1 ti leaf over another at right angles. Sprinkle vegetable mix in the center, then lay a mahi fillet on top of the vegetables. Spread a thin layer of herb sauce on fish and sprinkle with more vegetables. Place another fillet on top, spread with herb sauce, sprinkle with vegetables. Finish with a third fillet that is topped with herb sauce, vegetable mix, and a sprinkle of mushrooms. Season with salt and pepper to taste.

Gather up ti leaves to make a purse around fish and tie tightly with string just above bundle. Repeat for all four portions, using a fourth of the vegetables, a fourth of the mushrooms, and three mahi fillets for each lau lau. Steam for 8 to 10 minutes.

Sam's Place:
Birthplace of the Stew Omelet

In 1981, our family opened up a little hole-in-the-wall restaurant we called Sam's Place, next door to my dad's store in Laie. It was named after my father and run by my sister, Wai Sun, whom I had persuaded to return home from Maui, where she had been working as a chef at the Maui Marriott.

Although modest, it was a very adventurous enterprise in many respects. We had been born and raised in Laie, but we still put in a lot of thought before opening. We surveyed an area some nine miles toward Punaluu and another nine miles toward the Kuilima resort. We wanted to see what kinds of restaurants were available and what kind of food people wanted to eat. The verdict was clear—local food all the way!

Probably the most important thing about Sam's Place is that it was the place where we introduced our style of cooking to the public for the first time—local-style beef stews, chicken hekka, shoyu chicken, chicken tofu, pork tofu, char siu chicken, baked chicken, and breakfast items such as pancakes and omelets.

So much of the flavors—as well as the generous portions—we are known for today go back to the family-style meals we served at home and then refined at Sam's Place. Our diner in Kona, located in the bowling alley, with its paper plates and such, is actually similar to what we had at the original Sam's Place. It just gets a bit fancier at the restaurant.

We left the operation of Sam's Place in Laie in 1991, after ten years, because our work in Kona got too busy. The old restaurant is now operated by our cousin's family, and has been renamed the Hukilau Cafe.

Although his name may not be on the old restaurant anymore, it was there that my dad inspired our popular stew omelet. He worked hard, and one of his favorite quick meals was to put some rice in a bowl, pour beef stew over the rice, and throw two eggs on top. I thought about that and said, "What if we put a flat, frittata-like omelet over the rice, then pour the stew on top?" The ultimate stew omelet was born. I know it piques people's curiosity when they hear about it or see it on the menu. They wonder, "Stew omelet? How do you make a stew omelet?" Then, when they see it, they say, "Hey, that's how I eat at home!" Yeah, real Hawaiian-style grinds, that's part of the legacy of Sam's Place.

PAN-FRIED ONAGA
WITH FRESH DILL CREAM

SERVES 4

One of the reasons fish tastes so good when I cook it is that I sear in the flavor on high heat, Chinese style, and use a combination of cooking oil and butter for rich flavor. But you've got to be careful because butter burns easily. One way to keep it from burning is to heat the oil first, then the butter, and add the fish the moment the butter melts. You've got to keep your eye on it, though, or it will burn. A less risky way is to use clarified butter which doesn't burn as easily. To make clarified butter, you melt it, then pour the clear oily part off the top and store in your refrigerator until ready to use. The solid fatty particles that are left in the bottom of the pan are what cause it to burn. When cooking fish, it is best to sear in the flavor on medium-high heat, then reduce the heat to finish it, if necessary, although most fish is done as soon as the outside is seared. I recommend you use this searing method for all my fish recipes that involve frying or sautéing, but that is merely a suggestion. You are the creator, and you can use whatever method you prefer.

4	onaga fillets (6 oz. each), or any other snapper
1/2	cup flour, to dust fish
2	Tbsp. olive oil
2	Tbsp. butter
1	cup shiitake mushrooms, sliced
2	cups heavy cream
1	Tbsp. shoyu
2	Tbsp. fresh dill, chopped

salt and pepper to taste

SEASON fish fillets with salt and pepper and dust with flour.

Heat oil and butter in pan. Place fish skin side down and fry 2-1/2 to 3 minutes until golden brown. Turn and fry another 2 or 3 minutes, just until fish turns opaque in the middle. Remove fish and keep warm without overcooking.

Extract all but 2 tablespoons of oil from pan, add shiitake mushrooms, heavy cream, and shoyu. Bring to a boil. Reduce heat and simmer 3 or 4 minutes, or until sauce has been reduced to a nice consistency. Fold in fresh dill at the very end and adjust seasonings with salt and pepper.

Serve the sauce on the side, or pour sauce on plate and lay fish on top. This goes great with *Parsley Boiled Potatoes*.

SAUTÉED ISLAND FISH TRIO

SERVES 4

Living in Hawai'i we're fortunate to be able to catch and eat some of the best-eating fish in the world: opah, au, mahimahi, ono, ahi, opakapaka, onaga, uku, and so on. These fish are firm, moist, and have a mild flavor that makes them taste real good. That's why I like to feature fresh fish in my restaurants and cookbooks. Of all the different fish, my favorites are mahi, ahi, and opakapaka.

1   cup each of 5 of your favorite stir-fried vegetables, julienned
5   Tbsp. butter
3   Tbsp. olive oil
1/2 tsp. garlic, minced
salt and pepper to taste
4   fillets opakapaka (2 oz. each)
4   fillets mahimahi (2 oz. each)
4   fillets ahi (2 oz. each)
1/2 cup flour to dust fish

GARNISH:
4   sprigs of fresh parsley, or sprigs of your favorite fresh herbs

SAUCE:
1   Tbsp. shoyu
2   cups heavy cream
1   Tbsp. ginger, minced
1   cup shiitake mushrooms, sliced
salt and pepper to taste

YOU can use whatever vegetables you like. A few suggestions are carrots, red bell peppers, yellow bell peppers, onions, mushrooms, celery, zucchini, purple cabbage, and wonbok (napa) cabbage. The idea is to make a colorful mix.

Heat 2 tablespoons butter and 1 tablespoon olive oil and sauté vegetables and garlic for 2 minutes. Season with salt and pepper. Remove from pan, set aside and keep warm.

In pan combine cream and mushrooms. Bring to a boil, then reduce heat to a low simmer. Add ginger, shoyu, and salt and pepper. Simmer for another 3 or 4 minutes, or until the sauce is reduced to the consistency you like. Keep warm.

Lightly season fish with salt and pepper and dust with flour. Heat 3 tablespoons butter and 2 tablespoons olive oil in large sauté pan. Cook fish until medium rare, about 1-1/2 minutes per side.

Divide vegetables into four equal portions and mound one portion in the middle of each plate. Arrange 1 fillet each of the three different types of island fish around the side of the vegetable mound in a sort of pyramid fashion. Pour sauce around the edge and garnish with a sprig of parsley or other fresh herbs.

CRUSTED MAHIMAHI WITH
COCONUT CREAM SPINACH SAUCE

SERVES 4

This dish came from taking a traditional local cooking method that was used on festive occasions and shaking it up to bring it to the everyday household. I think I've made it simple enough so that people can do it at home.

4   mahimahi fillets (6 oz. each)
salt and pepper to taste
3   Tbsp. flour for dusting
2   eggs, lightly beaten
1   Tbsp. olive oil
3   Tbsp. butter

CRUST:

1/2   cup macadamia nuts,
      finely chopped
1/4   cup toasted sesame seeds
1/2   cup panko or bread crumbs

COCONUT CREAM
SPINACH SAUCE:

2   cups fresh spinach, chopped
3   Tbsp. butter
1   medium onion, minced
1   cup heavy cream
2   cups canned coconut milk
    (unsweetened)
2   Tbsp. cornstarch mixed
    with 1-1/2 tbsp. water,
    if needed for thickening
salt and pepper to taste

LIGHTLY season fish with salt and pepper and dust with flour. Combine macadamia nuts, toasted sesame seeds, and panko, and mix well. Dip just one side of floured mahi fillet in egg wash, let excess egg drip off, then dip into crust mixture and firmly press onto fish. I like to crust just one side of the fish because it makes for a nice contrast in textures—crisp on one side and moist on the other. You don't feel like you're getting too much batter. You want to taste the fish.

In large frying pan, heat oil and butter. Make sure it's hot before adding fish. Cook with the crust side down until golden brown, about 1-1/2 minutes (keep a close eye on it—mac nuts can brown very quickly), then turn and cook the other side about 1-1/2 minutes. Remove from pan, set aside and keep warm without over cooking.

In the same pan, add spinach, butter, and onions and cook for 1-1/2 to 2 minutes, until onions become translucent. Add heavy cream. Bring to a boil, reduce heat and simmer for 1 to 2 minutes. Add coconut milk. Cook for another 2 minutes. If sauce is thin, don't panic, all you need to do is add cornstarch mixture to the simmering sauce and cook for another minute. Adjust seasoning with salt and pepper.

Serve fish crust side up on mixed stir-fried vegetables, or on pasta, or garlic mashed potatoes, with sauce around the edge. Don't pour sauce over crust—it will make it soggy.

The Lure of the Sea

We're fortunate to live in Hawai'i, where we are surrounded by the sea and have access to some of the freshest seafood in the world. I love serving fresh hirame (flounder), golden tilapia and ogo (seaweed) raised at the aquaculture facility in Keahole, Kona. We are also blessed with a ready supply of freshly caught fish, thanks to an experienced network of dozens of independent fishermen from all over the Big Island. As long as they have a license, they know that they can call me anytime. With the advent of cellular telephones, they call me while they're still out at sea to tell me what they've got. I say, "Sure, bring it in," and they come straight to the restaurant. You can't get it any fresher.

When I think about fishing in Kona, I have to brag about my good friend Mark Santiago. Born and raised in Wahiawa, Mark moved to Kona in 1981, mainly to go fishing, I think. We got to know each other through a mutual friend. Working out of the basement at his home in Kalaoa, not far from where I live, Mark manufactures world-class PILI fishing lures. Whenever I want to just relax and get away from the pressures of work, I often hang out with Mark at his place.

I really respect Mark and what he's worked hard to accomplish. He left a steady job to pursue his dream some ten years ago when he purchased a small company called Pacific Island Lure Innovations (PILI). At the time, the company had a single product and produced about 25 handmade lures a week.

Facing a back order of more than 7,000 lures, Mark struggled for several years, barely able to keep up. Slowly, however, he developed PILI designs in varying sizes—1-1/4, 3-1/2, 4-1/2 and 6-1/2 inch models—to fit different needs and fishing conditions.

It's amazing to see how he does it. Each lure starts as a blank piece of foam. Mark shapes 'em, molds 'em, spray paints 'em by hand, using a tem-

plate. Then he caps and resins 'em. He knows how to play hard, too, and that's why I like him. I can drop in on him, shoot the breeze, have a few laughs, lose the stress.

Today, PILI is the premier lure manufacturer in Hawai'i, with products distributed all over the U.S. mainland and Alaska, throughout the South Pacific, Guam, New Zealand, Asia, Australia, and even in Europe. They are capable of cranking out 200 hand-crafted lures a day, averaging about 10,000 each year.

PILI competes with the big, major manufacturers who can mass-produce their lures via plastic injection processes, relying on equipment that costs hundreds of thousands of dollars. PILI lures are entirely handmade, so it's a struggle to meet the demand. If you consider imitation as being the sincerest form of flattery, PILI has had more than its share of flattery. The inferior quality of the imitation stuff shows, however, and in my book there is only one, the original, PILI.

The way I see it, Mark is the PILI king because he'll never put out anything inferior. He works and works at it until he's totally satisfied, and, to me, that's the sign of a professional. He never sits idle, either. Every time I visit him, he'll say, "Hey, Sam, come check this out." And he'll show me something new he's got going. Mark now produces a line of 20 different items, each taking months, or in some cases years, to develop. He takes the time to talk story with the fishermen and really listens to what they have to say. Then he develops a prototype, tests it, and refines it until he's got it working just so.

The last time I saw Mark, he was working on a rubber version of the basic PILI. He believes it will be more durable than the present foam and resin version and feel more "real" to the fish when they grab on to it. It could be made faster and cheaper too, giving consumers a quality PILI brand product at a more affordable price.

I don't think you could find a boat in Kona that doesn't have at least a few PILI lures on board. In fact, it's a common saying among local fishermen, whenever the fish aren't biting: "It's time to bring out the PILI's!"

Mark's an avid fisherman, a true craftsman, a close friend, and he makes an excellent poke. A little on the hot side, but, whooo-a, he does make a good poke!

BAKED LOCAL BOY MAHIMAHI
IN TI LEAVES

SERVES 4 TO 6

One of the more interesting things about cooking mahimahi is catching mahimahi. We go out about 30 or 40 miles from the north shore of Oahu and look for cargo nets or other floating debris. Once we find that, I can guarantee you we will find a school of succulent mahimahi feeding on the smaller fish that feed on the little fish and creatures that live in the flotsam. Mahi are beautiful fish—bright shiny blue, and bluish-green, with yellow spots. They average 22 to 44 pounds, and you can tell the bulls by their big round heads. It's a great fish to work with, just a center bone with lots of fillet. And it tastes great, mild and moist. My favorite way to cook it is baked "local boy" style in ti leaves.

6	ti leaves (may substitute corn husks, or tin foil)
1	slab or fillet of fresh mahimahi (3 to 4 lbs.)
1-1/2	cup mayonnaise
1/2	cup crab meat
1-1/2	Tbsp. shoyu
2	cups assorted colorful stir-fry vegetables, julienned
1	cup shiitake mushrooms, sliced
salt and pepper to taste	

PREHEAT oven to 350 degrees. You want to use a large baking dish that has a lid for this recipe, if you have it. If not, you can cover the dish with foil. Line the bottom of the dish with 3 ti leaves.

Lightly season fish with salt and pepper. Smear 1/2 cup of mayonnaise all over the fish. Lay fish on ti leaves in the baking dish. Mix the remaining mayonnaise with the crab meat and shoyu. Salt and pepper to taste. Spread this mixture over the top of the fish. Layer the julienned raw vegetables and shiitake mushrooms over that. Cover with remaining ti leaves, then cover with lid, or tightly seal with foil.

Bake in preheated oven for 35 to 45 minutes. Check after 35 minutes. It's done as soon as fish turns opaque in the middle. If it flakes with a fork, it is too well done.

A lot of people don't think they like fish because they've only eaten fish that's been overcooked. But when they come to my restaurant and try it, they go nuts it's so good!

POACHED SALMON
WITH TROPICAL FRUIT SALSA

SERVES 4

Seasoning is important, but you have to make sure you don't overseason. Most of my recipes call for salt and pepper to taste, but even if I forget to mention it here or there, you should still do it. I am known for blending small amounts of various spices in interesting ways so that the seasoning enhances rather than overpowers the food. I never use MSG—it's not necessary. The proper use of seasoning is to guide the natural flavors and bring out the best. For example, a little sugar added to something salty doesn't make it taste sweet, it just brings the flavor to a peak and rounds it out. Fresh herbs make a big difference and should always be added at the end of cooking, as their flavor evaporates if cooked too long. We're lucky in Hawai'i to have various fresh fruits throughout the year, and those flavors, combined with the distinct taste of salmon, makes for a very interesting dish.

8	salmon fillets (3 oz. each)

sprigs of fresh herbs for garnish

POACHING WATER:

4	cups water
1/2	cup Chinese parsley, chopped
2	cups white wine
1	cup mixture of carrots, onions, and celery, diced

Juice of 1 lemon

1	tsp. salt
1/2	tsp. cracked pepper

SALSA:

1	cup mangoes or lychee, or seasonal tropical fruit, diced
1	cup papaya, diced
1	cup pineapple, diced
1/2	cup Chinese parsley
1/4	cup red bell pepper, diced
1/4	cup tomatoes, diced

salt and pepper to taste

1	tsp. cumin
1/2	tsp. hot red pepper flakes

BLEND together all salsa ingredients and let sit at room temperature for 30 minutes.

Mix poaching water ingredients and bring to a boil. Poach salmon about 3 to 4 minutes, depending on thickness of fillets. As soon as salmon turns opaque in the middle, it's done. Myself, I like to leave the fish a little raw in the middle—it seems to taste better.

Divide the salsa into 4 portions. On each plate place a layer of salsa, 2 fish fillets, and a dollop of salsa on top of fish.

Garnish with a sprig of the fresh herb of your choice.

CALAMARI TARO CAKES

SERVES 6

If you've never tasted calamari, you ought to give it a try. A member of the squid family, it has a mild flavor, a nice firm texture, and is very economical.

2   lbs. calamari tentacles
enough water to cover
enough salt to make water salty
1-1/2 cups boiled sweet potatoes, mashed
1/2   cups taro, steamed and mashed
salt and pepper to taste
1   tsp. Chinese parsley, minced
1   Tbsp. melted butter
2   eggs
6   slices bacon, finely chopped
2   Tbsp. flour, or more, as needed
1/2   cup clarified butter
1/2   cup olive oil

BRING salted water to a boil, drop in tentacles and cook for about 1 minute. Rinse in cold water. Chop coarsely and blend well with sweet potatoes, taro, salt and pepper, Chinese parsley, melted butter, and eggs. Brown bacon and fold into mixture.

Divide into 12 equal portions, roll into balls and flatten into cakes. Dust with flour and fry until golden brown in clarified butter and olive oil. The cakes can also be deep-fried (at 350 to 375 degrees) after being dipped into beaten eggs, then bread crumbs.

I like going out in the ocean late at night and seeing all the calamari swimming around the lights. They are so easy to catch. Just throw in a glow-stick attached to a hook and all of a sudden you've got a bunch of calamari.

DEEP-FRIED CALAMARI WITH GINGER PESTO

SERVES 4

This is really good. If you've never had it before, it's like eating a great potato chip—moist on the inside, crunchy on the outside. Calamari (squid) is a really mild seafood. Because of its appearance you wouldn't think it would taste good, but it really is tasty. Ginger pesto marries well with squid.

12	medium calamari
2	Tbsp. shoyu
salt and pepper to taste	
2	cups cornstarch
enough oil for deep-fat frying	

GINGER PESTO:

1/2	cup Chinese parsley, minced
1/2	cup green onions, minced
1/4	cup ginger, minced
salt and white pepper to taste	
3/4	cups salad oil

CLEAN calamari, cut into 1/2-inch rings. Season with shoyu, salt and pepper to taste, then let sit for about an hour.

Mix all pesto ingredients until well blended and set aside.

Drain calamari and roll in cornstarch until coated. Deep-fry for about 2 or 3 minutes, until golden brown.

Toss with *Ginger Pesto* in a mixing bowl and serve on a bed of young, tender lettuce leaves.

CALAMARI STIR-FRY

SERVES 4

12	medium calamari
4	cups of your five favorite stir-fry vegetables, julienned
2	Tbsp. olive oil
1	Tbsp. butter

MARINADE:

1	cup shoyu
1	cup oil
4	Tbsp. mirin
1	tsp. sesame oil
4	Tbsp. Chinese parsley, minced
2	Tbsp. garlic, minced
2	Tbsp. ginger, minced
1	tsp. salt
1/2	tsp. white pepper
2	Tbsp. green onions, thinly sliced
4	Tbsp. cornstarch
3	tsp. brown sugar

TERIYAKI GLAZE:

1/2	cup shoyu
1/4	cup mirin
1/4	cup water
2	Tbsp. brown sugar
1	tsp. garlic, minced
1	tsp. ginger, minced
1/2	tsp. hot red pepper flakes
1	Tbsp. cornstarch blended with 2 Tbsp. water to make a smooth paste

CLEAN calamari, cut into 1/2-inch rings. Combine marinade ingredients and marinate calamari rings for 1 hour.

In a saucepan, bring all *Teriyaki Glaze* ingredients (except for cornstarch/water mixture) to a boil, then stir in cornstarch mixture. Reduce heat and simmer, stirring frequently, until thickened.

Heat oil and butter in a large pan or wok and stir-fry calamari real quick— just a minute, or maybe a minute and a half. You just want to sizzle it real quick. Remove from pan. Add vegetables and stir-fry 2 to 3 minutes. Add Teriyaki Glaze, then fold in calamari. You can either serve it with hot steamed rice as a full meal, or just by itself as a pupu. If you plan to serve this to guests and want to "wow" them a little, you can prepare all the ingredients ahead of time, then stir-fry everything in a portable wok right at the table. This adds a lot of show and will have your guests "ooohing" and "aahing."

This is the fastest and easiest stir-fry you can ever make and one of the tastiest. Squid is also the most economical seafood you can buy.

LAIE SEAFOOD QUICHE

SERVES 4 TO 6

If you like quiche, this is a very interesting one. I named it after Laie because that's the fishing village where I was raised by fishermen. I want to give them some credit. I like working with quiche because it's quick and easy and delicious.

9-in. **pastry crust, partially baked (350 degrees for about 5 minutes)**

2 **Tbsp. butter**

6 **green onions, thinly sliced**

2 **Tbsp. tomatoes, diced**

1 **cup shiitake mushrooms, sliced**

2 **cups combination of crabmeat, scallops, shrimp, mahimahi chunks, ono chunks**

3 **eggs**

1-1/2 **cups heavy cream**

salt and white pepper to taste

2 **Tbsp. fresh dill**

3-1/2 **oz. grated Gruyere cheese, or Monterey Jack, or cheddar, or a combination of cheeses**

IN a large skillet, sauté green onions, tomatoes and mushrooms for 1 to 2 minutes in the butter. Add all the seafood and stir-fry for about 4 or 5 minutes, until done. Place in colander and drain completely.

Whisk together eggs, cream, salt and white pepper, until well blended. Add dill and mix well, then set aside.

Spoon seafood into pie crust and cover with egg and cream mixture. You may have to use a fork to readjust the seafood to make sure it is evenly distributed. Sprinkle cheese on top.

Place quiche pan on a cookie sheet and bake in a 350-degree preheated oven for about 45 minutes, maximum. Check after 35 minutes by inserting a knife into the center. When the knife comes out clean, the quiche is done.

STEAMED OPAH
(MOONFISH)

SERVES 4

Opah, or moonfish, was for a long time a very underrated fish, but in the early 1970s it started to catch on and began to come of age in the '80s. It runs from 60 to 250 pounds and is caught in very deep water by the same boats that catch ahi. Its body is round, almost like a big sunfish, but more full-bodied. It looks like a huge overgrown piranha, without teeth. It's an interesting fish because it has three different types of meat that are different in color, flavor, and texture. The backstrap, which is generally the only part of the fish you can buy in the store, is a nice, light-pink snapper color, while the flanks above the stomach are real oily and almost the same orange color as salmon; they are best steamed. The cheek meat is red like yellowfin tuna and is great for stir-frying.

4   opah fillets (6 oz. each)
salt and pepper to taste
3   Tbsp. olive oil
2   Tbsp. white wine

GINGER PESTO:
1   Tbsp. Chinese parsley, minced
1   Tbsp. green onions, minced
1   Tbsp. ginger, minced
1-1/2 Tbsp. light salad oil
salt and white pepper to taste

GINGER CREAM SAUCE:
2   cups heavy cream
1   cup shiitake mushrooms, sliced
1   Tbsp. shoyu
1   Tbsp. fresh ginger root, sliced thinly, then finely julienned into shreds
1   Tbsp. Chinese parsley, minced
salt and white pepper to taste

TO prepare this dish you need a steamer, or you can improvise like the Chinese do with a regular covered pot into which you put a bowl upside down with a plate on top.

Season the opah with salt and pepper and marinate in the olive oil and wine for 20 to 30 minutes.

Mix *Ginger Pesto* ingredients. Arrange the fish in your steamer and spread about 1 teaspoon of pesto on each fillet. Steam for 6 to 8 minutes, or until done.

Serve on top of a dollop of *Garlic Mashed Potatoes* (see recipe under *Sam's Favorite Side Dishes*), surrounded by *Ginger Cream Sauce*.

To make the sauce, combine cream, mushrooms, shoyu and ginger. Bring to a boil, lower heat and let simmer until reduced to the consistency you prefer. Fold in Chinese parsley and adjust seasonings with salt and white pepper.

• SAM'S AMAZING NO-FAT STEAMED FISH AND VEGETABLES

SERVES 1

My life-time battle has always been with my weight, so I can relate to others who have this problem. It's tough. I'm always trying to come up with recipes that cut calories without cutting taste, and people are always asking me for this, but I think the main problem is that things that taste really good are usually fattening. This recipe of steamed fish and vegetables seasoned with fresh herbs is as delicious as food can be without added fat.

2	pieces of uku (3 oz. each), or salmon
2	fresh broccoli florets
2	fresh cauliflower florets
4	stalks fresh asparagus
2	shiitake mushrooms
1/2	red bell pepper, sliced
salt and pepper to taste	
1	medium ginger finger, sliced very thin, then finely julienned into hair-thin shreds
a sprig of fresh dill	
1	Tbsp. shoyu (optional)

ARRANGE fish and vegetables in steamer basket, or on a plate in an impromptu steamer (a pot in which you've placed a bowl up-side-down with a plate on top). Season with salt and pepper and sprinkle with ginger. Lay a sprig of ginger on top of fish. Steam for 6 to 8 minutes, or until done. This dish is just as good hot or cold. You can drizzle it with a little shoyu, if you like.

HILO GINGER LOBSTER

SERVES 2

1	lobster (2 to 3 lbs.), cut up, claws cracked
1	Tbsp. minced pork
2	Tbsp. olive oil
2	Tbsp. butter
1	large finger ginger, finely julienned
1	tsp. garlic, minced
4	cups combination of your five favorite vegetables, julienned
1-1/2	cups chicken broth or stock
2	whole eggs, whipped
3	Tbsp. cornstarch mixed with
2-1/2	Tbsp. water, for thickening
4	sprigs fresh Chinese parsley, for garnish

SET aside 1 teaspoon of ginger to use as garnish.

Stir-fry pork, ginger, and garlic in hot oil and butter for 1 minute. Add lobster and cook 2 minutes more. Add vegetables and broth. As soon as it boils, whisk in eggs, then add cornstarch mixture. Lower heat and simmer 2 to 3 minutes, then remove from pan. Total cooking time shouldn't be more than 5 or 6 minutes.

Garnish with sprigs of Chinese parsley and ginger.

When you drive along the Hamakua Coast to Hilo from Kona and get about three-quarters of the way there, right around Pepeekeo, you look on the sides of the mountains and see cultivated ginger growing everywhere. It gets a chef excited to see all that fresh ginger, knowing all the great dishes he can make with it. Ginger gives you instant flavor, and that's important when you're cooking something like lobster that you have to cook quickly and can't simmer together with seasonings for a long time.

STUFFED HUALALAI LOBSTER

SERVES 2

1   lobster (2 to 3 lbs.),
      cleaned and rinsed

STUFFING:

1-1/2 cups butter

1-1/2 cups fresh mushrooms,
      finely chopped

1/2   Tbsp. shallots,
      or white onion, minced

1/2   cup bread crumbs

1   Tbsp. red bell pepper, diced

1/2   cup grated Parmesan
      cheese

1   tsp. parsley, chopped

salt and pepper to taste

HEAT butter. Add mushrooms and shallots and stir-fry 4 to 5 minutes, until mushrooms are nicely browned. Add bread crumbs and peppers. Cook another 2 minutes, then set aside. When cooled to room temperature, fold in Parmesan and parsley. Adjust seasoning with salt and pepper.

Crack lobster claws and slit lobster down the back, being careful not to cut all the way through. Spread stuffing in slit and bake in a 350-degree oven 15 to 20 minutes. The lobster is done when the meat turns from translucent to opaque.

When you're diving in Hawai'i you always find lobsters hiding in cracks and crevices in the reefs and under rock overhangs. These are spiny lobsters. They don't have claws. They have big heads and little tails, unlike cold water lobsters which have claws, small heads, and big tails. Spinies are sweeter, though, and more tender. It's real important not to overcook lobster—it makes it rubbery and tough.

TAHITIAN COLD LOBSTER

SERVES 1

Lobster always excites people, however it's served. This particular cold presentation is as dramatic as it is delicious and is something that can be prepared ahead of time and held in the fridge. People can't believe how good it is. It's real simple to do, but it looks like it took a long time and a lot of trouble.

1	lobster (1-1/2 lbs.)
	Juice of 1 lemon
1	tsp. cracked peppercorns
2	bay leaves
1	clove garlic, crushed
1	beer
2	Tbsp. asparagus, chopped (parboil until tender before chopping)
2	Tbsp. green peas
2	Tbsp. carrots, diced (parboiled 2-3 minutes)
1/2	tsp. Chinese parsley, minced
1/2	tsp. fresh dill
1/2	cup fresh spinach, chopped (or frozen cooked spinach, squeezed)
2	Tbsp. water chestnuts, diced
	salt and pepper, to taste
1	cup mayonnaise, or to taste
1/2	tsp. curry powder, or to taste

GARNISHES:

lemon wedges

fresh dill sprig

STEAM lobster for 6 to 8 minutes over boiling water to which you have added lemon juice, cracked peppercorns, bay leaves, garlic, and beer. Remove lobster from steamer when cooked and immediately submerge in ice water. Let remain in ice water until chilled, about 15 to 20 minutes.

While lobster cools, make the salad by mixing all remaining ingredients, except for the mayonnaise and curry powder. Blend mayonnaise and curry powder together, then mix thoroughly with vegetables.

Split the lobster in two, remove tail meat, discard innards, and reserve shell. Fill shell about half full with salad mix, reserving about 1/2 cup of the mix. Slice tail meat into 3 or 4 sections and replace in tail over salad, leaving gaps between sections to be filled with reserved salad mix. Crack claws and use for garnish.

Arrange stuffed lobster and cracked claws on bed of finely chopped lettuce and garnish with lemon wedges and a sprig of fresh dill.

BLACK BEAN DUNGENESS CRAB

SERVES 1 TO 2

Fermenting black beans is the first stage of making shoyu. When soy beans ferment, they turn black and shouldn't be confused with those little, dried black beans used in Hispanic cookery. You don't have to use a lot for this dish—they're very salty. Fermented black soy beans enhance the sweetness and flavor of crab, but you don't want to overwhelm, so use just a little.

1	whole 3-lb. Dungeness crab
3	Tbsp. oil
1/2	cup fresh ginger, julienned
2	cups chicken broth
1/2	tsp. hot red pepper flakes (optional)
2	Tbsp. fermented black beans (look in Oriental section of supermarket)
1	tsp. sugar
1-1/2	Tbsp. cornstarch mixed with
2	Tbsp. water
4	green onions, julienned
1	Tbsp. Chinese parsley, chopped
1	Tbsp. butter

RINSE crab. Remove the top shell and separate the claws from the body, discarding head and innards. Crack the claws and quarter the body.

Heat oil and stir-fry crab with half the ginger for 1 minute. Add half the broth and the pepper flakes (if you want it spicy). Cover and steam for 5 minutes. Remove crab to a heated serving platter.

Add remaining broth, the black beans, and the sugar, and bring to a boil. Blend cornstarch with water to make a smooth paste and stir into broth. Reduce heat and simmer, stirring frequently, until thickened. Stir in remaining ginger, green onions, and Chinese parsley. Fold in butter. Pour over crab and serve immediately.

ISLAND SEAFOOD STEW

SERVES 6

This recipe is great for when you don't have a lot of one thing for a meal, but have a little of several different things. It's the same basic idea as cioppino or bouillabaisse, but uses different ingredients and seasonings, so you get a different taste.

1-1/2	lbs. opah, opakapaka, mahimahi, or firm white fish of your choice
1/2	lb. shrimp (21-25 ct.) or lobster
3	cups clam juice
3-1/2	cups chicken broth
1	cup white wine
	juice of 1 lemon
2	Tbsp. tomato paste
1/2	lb. clams or mussels
1/2	cup olive oil
1	large onion, diced
1	cup celery, thinly sliced
1	cup carrots, diced

1/2	cup sweet potatoes, parboiled 5 to 6 minutes and cubed
1/2	cup taro, parboiled 5 to 6 minutes and cubed
1	Tbsp. garlic, minced
1	tomato, diced
1/4	tsp. red pepper flakes, or 1 Hawaiian chili pepper, chopped
1	cup fresh basil, chopped
2	bay leaves
	pinch of saffron
1/2	cup Chinese parsley, chopped

CUT fish into 1-inch cubes. Shell and devein shrimp.

In a large pot, combine clam juice, chicken broth, white wine, lemon juice, and tomato paste and bring to a boil. Add shrimp and return to boil. Remove shrimp and set aside.

Return stock to a boil, add fish and clams or mussels. Remove from heat and let stand 2 minutes. Remove seafood from stock and set aside.

In a skillet, heat olive oil and sauté onion, celery, carrots, sweet potatoes, taro, and garlic for 2 minutes. Add onion mixture to stock. Add remaining ingredients and simmer for 15 minutes. Stir in seafood. Serve hot.

GINGER BOILED FRESH SHRIMP WITH MY DAD'S FAVORITE DIPPING SAUCE

SERVES 1 TO 2

This dish is best when you use the freshest shrimp, right out of the ocean. You poach them by dropping them into boiling ginger broth and then take them out the moment they turn pink. The dip brings out the sweetness of the shrimp. The fresher the shrimp, the sweeter they taste.

1   lb. shrimp (16-20 ct.), rinsed, with shells left on

POACHING WATER:

4   cups water
1   medium finger fresh ginger, crushed
1/2   cup Chinese parsley, chopped
2   cups white wine
1   cup mixture of carrots, onions, and celery, diced
juice of 1 lemon
1   tsp. salt
1/2   tsp. cracked pepper

MY DAD'S FAVORITE DIPPING SAUCE:

1/2   cup shoyu
2   tsp. sugar
1   tsp. salad oil
1/2   tsp. sesame oil
1   tsp. Chinese parsley, minced

MIX poaching water ingredients and bring to a boil. Add shrimp. As soon as it starts to boil again, remove shrimp. Don't overcook. Shrimp are cooked before they curl up, so remove them promptly. Serve with *My Dad's Favorite Dipping Sauce,* which you make as follows: Bring shoyu and sugar to a boil. Remove from heat and pour into a dip bowl. Heat the oil, then pour into shoyu mixture. Fold in Chinese parsley. If you like it spicy, you can throw in a whole red chili pepper when you heat the oil.

SHRIMP TEMPURA, SAM'S WAY

SERVES 4

I remember going to Japan and walking the streets of the Ginza with my good friend Dalton Tanonaka. He was explaining to me that the oil used in high-class tempura restaurants is used only once, just for you, then sold to other restaurants. This is one of the secrets of good tempura: always use fresh oil that you haven't cooked anything else in.

This recipe isn't limited to shrimp. You can use it also for chicken, fish, or vegetables. What makes this particular tempura dish different is my special dipping sauce, as well as the lacy effect you get by sprinkling batter on the surface of the hot oil before adding the shrimp.

2	lbs. shrimp, shelled and deveined
1	cup flour
1/2	cup rice flour
1	tsp. baking powder
1/2	cup cornstarch
1/4	tsp. salt
1-2/3	cups water
1	egg, beaten
enough fat or oil for deep-fat frying	

WHEN shelling shrimp, leave tails on. Butterfly shrimp by slicing down through the back, being careful not to cut in two. Flatten shrimps and lightly score underside diagonally to prevent curling.

Sift flours, baking powder, cornstarch, and salt together. Combine egg and water and mix thoroughly with dry ingredients.

Heat oil or fat to 365 degrees. Using your fingers, sprinkle a little of the batter on top of the hot oil. Repeat several times to make a lacy background, working rapidly. Dip 3 or 4 shrimp in batter and lay carefully on top of frying batter. Sprinkle more batter on top of shrimp. After 1 minute, turn shrimp. Cook until lightly browned, drain, and serve with my special sauce, or the dipping sauce of your choice.

SAM'S SPECIAL TEMPURA SAUCE:

2	cups dashi (look in Oriental section of your supermarket)
5	inches dashikonbu
1/2	cup bonito flakes
2	tsp. shoyu
1/2	tsp. salt
1/2	tsp. ginger, grated
1/2	tsp. sugar
1/2	cup turnip, grated
1	Tbsp. green onion, sliced
1 tsp. sesame pepper oil	

Add dashikonbu to boiling dashi and cook 10 minutes. Add bonito and sugar and boil 3 minutes. Remove from burner and strain. Add shoyu, salt, and ginger and bring to a boil. Cool, then add turnip, green onion, and sesame pepper oil.

NIHOA SHRIMP KABOBS

SERVES 4

24   large shrimp (16-20 ct.),
      shelled and deveined
      bamboo skewers

MARINADE:

1	cup oil
1	cup shoyu
2	tsp. sesame oil
4	Tbsp. mirin
2	Tbsp. garlic, minced
2	Tbsp. ginger, minced
1/2	tsp. salt
1/2	tsp. white pepper
1	Tbsp. brown sugar
1/2	tsp. hot peppers
1	tsp. Chinese parsley

PREPARE coals in hibachi.
Mix marinade ingredients.
Place shrimp on bamboo skewers
and marinate in mixture for 45 minutes to 1 hour.

Grill shrimp kabobs on hibachi
about 1-1/2 minutes per side. Shrimp
are done when they turn pink all
over. Don't over cook. You can serve
them with your favorite dipping
sauce, or try this one:

Blend well 1 teaspoon sugar, 1
teaspoon Chinese parsley, 2 teaspoons Hoisin sauce, 2 tablespoons
Chinese garlic chili sauce, and 4
tablespoons catsup.

*Catching deep-sea shrimp in Hawai'i is getting tougher and
tougher, because you have to go way down deep and drag the
bottom, which wipes out all the shrimp, and because it's so cold
and dark down there it takes years and years for the shrimp to
reproduce and make a comeback. Because of that, most shrimp
served in restaurants today in Hawaii have been raised on aquaculture farms. Some still come from places like Nihoa, though. A
few people can taste the difference, but most can't.*

PARADISE SHRIMP SCAMPI WITH DILL CREAM SAUCE OVER TARO PASTA

SERVES 4

Scampi is usually shrimp in butter and garlic. My variation uses cream with dill over pasta and fresh taro. It's a whole different take. Not your typical scampi. It's fun to make and even more fun to eat.

2   **lbs. large shrimp (16 to 20 ct.), peeled and deveined**

flour (enough to dust shrimp)

2   **Tbsp. olive oil**

1   **Tbsp. garlic, minced**

2   **Tbsp. butter**

2   **cups cooked taro, large dice**

1-1/2   **lbs. linguine, cooked and drained**

1   **Tbsp. shoyu**

5   **cups heavy cream (may need more)**

2   **Tbsp. fresh dill, minced**

salt and pepper to taste

4   **Tbsp. grated Parmesan cheese**

MARINADE:

1   **Tbsp. garlic, minced**

1   **Tbsp. olive oil**

salt and pepper to taste

MIX marinade ingredients and marinate shrimp 15 to 20 minutes.

Dust shrimp with flour and sear quickly in 2 tablespoons olive oil on medium-high heat for about 1 to 1-1/2 minutes. Remove from heat and set aside (shrimp will be raw on the inside).

Sauté 1 tablespoon minced garlic with cooked taro in butter. Add cooked linguine, shoyu and heavy cream, and bring to a rolling simmer. Continue simmering until thick,

about 3 or 4 minutes. You need to keep your eye on it. If the pasta absorbs a lot of the cream, you may have to add a little more cream. If you add more cream, continue to cook until reduced to a nice thick consistency. Add shrimp and dill and adjust seasoning with salt and pepper. Cook for another minute until shrimp is done, then fold in grated Parmesan cheese.

Serve in pasta bowls with fresh baked garlic bread and salad. Yummy!

MY KIDS' FAVORITE SEAFOOD LASAGNA IN WHITE SAUCE

SERVES 12 TO 20

If you give my kids a choice five nights a week, they'll say lasagna every night, whether it's with tomato sauce and cheese, or vegetables, or seafood. When I make seafood lasagna, they get the most excited. They like the big chunks of fish and shrimp and scallops in cream sauce with all that pasta and cheese. Man, that sounds so good, I think I'll go make some right now.

1 lb. lasagna noodles
oil
2 cups poached broccoli
2 cups poached zucchini
1 lb. fresh mahimahi fillets, 1/4-in. thick
1 lb. salmon fillets, 1/4-in. thick
1 lb. scallops
1 lb. bay shrimp
4 oz. Parmesan cheese, freshly grated
1 lb. Mozzarella cheese, grated

POACHING WATER:

1 tsp. ginger, minced
4 cups water
2 cups white wine
1 cup carrots, diced
1 cup onions, diced
1 cup celery, diced
juice of 1 lemon
1 tsp. salt
1/2 tsp. cracked pepper

CHEESE FILLING:

4 eggs
1 lb. ricotta cheese
salt and pepper to taste
2 Tbsp. dill, chopped fine
2 Tbsp. parsley, chopped

WHITE SAUCE:

8 Tbsp. butter
1/4 cup onion, minced
2 Tbsp. garlic, minced
6 Tbsp. flour
1 qt. milk

COOK lasagna noodles according to package directions. Rinse well and drain. Mix noodles gently with enough oil to keep them from sticking together. Set aside.

Poach broccoli and zucchini and set aside. Poach seafood for 2 minutes and remove from poaching water. Prepare cheese filling by beating eggs and mixing well with ricotta, salt and pepper, dill and parsley.

To make white sauce, first sauté 1/4 cup minced onion and 2 tablespoons minced garlic in 2 tablespoons butter and set aside. Melt 6 tablespoons of butter, then add 6 tablespoons of flour and cook on low heat for 10 minutes, stirring constantly—don't brown. Heat the milk until just before it boils, then pour over butter/flour mixture and stir vigorously until smooth. Add onions and garlic and simmer, uncovered, on low for 15 minutes. Adjust seasoning with salt and pepper.

Grease a large baking dish and spread a thin layer of white sauce on the bottom. Build the lasagna by alternating layers of noodles, cheese filling, seafood, sauce, mozzarella, and Parmesan. Reserve all the poached vegetables and some of the bay shrimp until the very end. For the top layer, proceed as for the other layers, then finish with a layer of poached vegetables and bay shrimp. Cover with remaining cream sauce, mozzarella and Parmesan.

SAM'S CLAMS WITH BLACK BEAN BUTTER

SERVES 2 CLAM LOVERS

24	clams rinsed and washed very clean
1	Tbsp. salad oil
1	medium finger of ginger, sliced thin
2	tsp. garlic, minced
2	Tbsp. Chinese fermented black beans
1	tsp. salt
3	Tbsp. shoyu
1-1/2	Tbsp. sake
1	tsp. sugar
2	cups chicken broth
1	Tbsp. butter
1-1/2	Tbsp. cornstarch mixed with
1	Tbsp. water
sprigs of Chinese parsley for garnish	

HEAT oil in skillet on medium-high. Sauté ginger and garlic with clams in shell until shells open and remove from heat. Mash beans and add salt, shoyu, sake, and sugar and mix well.

Add chicken broth and bean mixture to clams and bring to a boil. Reduce heat, cover and cook on medium until clams are done and open up. Then return to a boil. Add cornstarch mixture, simmer until thick, and fold in butter.

Garnish with sprigs of Chinese parsley.

I like cooking clams, not only because it's interesting to see the shells open up when you're cooking them, but because it makes for such a nice conversational food. It's great to sit there talking story while you're dipping sauce with the shell and sucking out the juicy meat. I guess you could say it's real sucking good. And when you blend it with black bean sauce, it's definitely a home run.

PASTA

CHINESE PASTA PRIMAVERA

SERVES 8

This is my way of blending both Chinese and Italian influences in a hearty pasta dish.

1	lb. linguine
1	medium red bell pepper, cut in strips
1	medium yellow bell pepper, cut in strips
2	medium zucchini, trimmed but not peeled, sliced
1/2	lb. broccoli florets
1/2	lb. fresh asparagus, cut in 1-in. pieces
1/2	lb. whole sugar snap peas, or Chinese snow peas
6	shallots or green onions, sliced thin
1	clove garlic, minced
1	Tbsp. butter
1	Tbsp. olive oil
1/4	cup Chinese parsley, chopped
2	Tbsp. Thai basil
1	Tbsp. shoyu
	salt and pepper to taste
1/4	cup Parmesan cheese, freshly grated

FILL a large pot with water and begin heating it for the pasta. Heat oil and butter in a large skillet or wok and stir-fry vegetables, onions, and garlic about 3 minutes. Add parsley and basil and cook another minute, or until vegetables are done to your taste—they should be a little crunchy.

When water boils, add linguine and cook according to package directions; it should be al dente. Season vegetables with salt and pepper, mix with shoyu, toss with pasta, and sprinkle with Parmesan.

Pasta is a very interesting dish. It is a trendy food of the 90s, while at the same time it is one of those classics that will never change. People like it, and it's healthy, simple, and satisfying. It's just water, salt, and flour, and sometimes eggs, and you can't get more basic than that. When Marco Polo toured China, he fell in love with noodles and brought the concept back to Italy. But when the Italians tried to make Chinese noodles, they had to use the flour and methods available in Italy, which were very different from those in China, and that's why Italian pasta is different from Chinese. But it's the same basic idea.

KONA FISHERMAN'S WIFE PASTA

SERVES 4 TO 6

1	lb. bow tie pasta
2-1/2	tsp. salt
30	fresh opal basil leaves, wiped clean with a soft cloth
1/2	cup Parmesan cheese, freshly grated
1	cup macadamia nuts, coarsely chopped
1/3	cup olive oil

HEAT water with 2 teaspoons salt in a large pot. While waiting for it to boil, place the basil, cheese, the remaining 1/2 teaspoon of salt and the nuts into a large mortar and pound to a pulp. Slowly add the olive oil, stirring. If you don't have a mortar, use a blender on low.

When the water boils, add the bow tie pasta. Stir to keep from sticking together and cook until it's al dente. Drain, then place pasta in large bowl and mix well with nut sauce. Serve at once.

HONAUNAU FARMER'S SPAGHETTI

SERVES 4

1	lb. spaghetti
4	Tbsp. oil
1	medium onion, julienned
2	cooked skinless chicken breasts, cut into thin strips
2/3	cups fresh mushrooms, thinly sliced
1	medium carrot, julienned
2	basil leaves, finely chopped
3	small ripe tomatoes, peeled, quartered, seeded, and cut into strips
3/4	cup whole Chinese sugar snap or snow peas
1	cup black olives, sliced
	salt and pepper to taste
3/4	cup Parmesan cheese, freshly grated

HEAT salted water for spaghetti. Cook onion and chicken in oil over medium heat about 3 or 4 minutes, or until onions are translucent and chicken loses its pink color. Add mushrooms and cook for 2 minutes over low heat. Add carrot, basil, and tomatoes, and simmer slowly for 15 minutes. Fold in peas and black olives and cook just until heated through.

Cook spaghetti the way you like it, drain, and turn onto a large preheated serving dish.

Pour the sauce over the spaghetti, add the Parmesan, mix well, and serve with a salad of fresh Honaunau lettuce and freshly baked garlic bread.

MANICOTTI KILAUEA

SERVES 8

1/2 lb. manicotti (16 shells), boiled and drained
freshly grated Parmesan cheese to taste

CHEESE FILLING:

1-1/2 lb. ricotta cheese

1/2 lb. Puna goat cheese, crumbled

1/2 lb. mozzarella cheese, grated

1 Tbsp. fresh dill, chopped

1 Tbsp. fresh Chinese parsley, chopped

1 tsp. Thai basil

1/2 tsp. salt

SAUSAGE AND ONO SAUCE:

1 lb. Italian sausage

1 lb. ono, diced, or firm mild fish of your choice

1 medium onion, minced

4 cups canned tomato purée

6 oz. canned tomato paste

1 cup water

1 tsp. opal basil

1 tsp. sugar

salt and pepper to taste

REMOVE skin from sausage. Place sausage in skillet and break up while browning well. Discard all but 1 tablespoon of fat and quickly sauté ono and onions, just until fish loses its translucency.

Stir in browned sausage, puréed tomato, tomato paste, opal basil, sugar, salt and pepper to taste, and the water. Cover and simmer on low for 45 minutes to 1 hour. Meanwhile, preheat oven to 375 degrees.

In a large bowl, combine ricotta, goat cheese, mozzarella, dill, Chinese parsley, Thai basil, and salt, and mix well. Stuff cooked manicotti shells with this filling.

Spoon half the sausage/ono sauce into one 13-by-9-inch baking dish, or into two 9-inch square baking dishes. Arrange half of the stuffed shells in one layer on top of the sauce. Spoon all but 3/4 cup of the remaining sauce over the shells, top with the rest of the shells in another layer. Finish with the 3/4 cup reserved sauce and sprinkle with Parmesan.

Bake for 30 minutes.

LUAU-STYLE
CHEESE CANNELLONI
SERVES 4

16   **large cannelloni**
1   **lb. luau (taro) leaves,**
     or fresh spinach
10   **oz. ricotta cheese**
2   **cups Parmesan cheese,**
     freshly grated
5   **oz. Puna goat cheese**
1/2   **tsp. garlic, minced**
1/3   **cup macadamia nuts,**
     chopped and toasted
salt and pepper to taste
2   **cups white sauce**
     (recipe follows)

HEAT plenty of salted water for pasta. When water boils, put in the cannelloni one at a time, stir, and cook over medium heat. When the cannelloni are half done (after 5 or 6 minutes for commercial pasta or 2 minutes for fresh pasta), remove and plunge into cold water. Drain and spread out on cloth towels.

Prepare luau (taro) leaves by parboiling for 8 minutes. Drain in a sieve, squeeze dry, and chop very fine. If using spinach, cook 2 minutes, drain and squeeze dry, and chop very fine.

While the pasta is cooking, put the chopped taro leaves or spinach into a bowl. Mix well with the ricotta, about half the Parmesan, the goat cheese, garlic, half of the toasted macadamia nuts, and salt and pepper to taste.

Preheat the oven to 350 degrees. Butter thoroughly an ovenproof dish large enough to hold the cannelloni in a single layer. Fill the cannelloni with the spinach/cheese/nut mixture and arrange in dish. Sprinkle with remaining Parmesan and cover with white sauce. Sprinkle with remaining toasted macadamia nuts.

Bake for about 20 minutes, or until the sauce is bubbling and the surface is lightly colored. Serve immediately.

WHITE SAUCE
2   **Tbsp. butter**
2   **Tbsp. flour**
2-1/2 cups half and half
salt and white pepper to taste
1/2   **cup macadamia nuts,**
     chopped and toasted

Melt butter in a heavy saucepan over low heat. Stir in the flour and cook gently, stirring, for 2 or 3 minutes. Pour in half and half all at once, whisking constantly to blend until smooth. Increase heat and continue whisking while sauce comes to a boil.

Reduce heat to very low and simmer, uncovered, for about 15 minutes, stirring occasionally to prevent sauce from developing a top skin or sticking to bottom of pan. Season with salt and pepper. Fold in macadamia nuts, reserving 2 tablespoons for sprinkling over top of cannelloni. Whisk again until the sauce is smooth.

Makes two cups.

CLASSICS SAM CHOY STYLE

Some of these recipes have been in my family for generations, handed down from my great-grandparents, grandparents, and parents, and I know I'll pass them on to my kids because even today these dishes are still able to light people up. I'm Hawaiian and Chinese, and what I cook has been handed down on both sides of the family. My mom's mom, my *tutu*, was trained in England after being hand-picked to serve Hawaiian royalty. That's where some of the traditional European cookery came in. I call these recipes classics because they are timeless comfort foods. They are dishes that excited me when I was growing up. They are special to me, foods that I hold close to my heart.

HAWAIIAN PRIME RIB AU JUS

SERVES 14 TO 20

14-lb. standing rib roast
10   garlic cloves, crushed
2   Tbsp. salt mixed with
     1 Tbsp. cracked pepper
     and 2 Tbsp. garlic salt
2   Tbsp. rosemary mixed with
     1 tsp. thyme
2   cups carrots, chunked
2   cups celery, chunked
2   cups onions, chunked
1   qt. chicken broth
1   qt. beef broth
1   cup cornstarch mixed
     with 1/2 cup water
salt and pepper to taste

PREHEAT oven to 350 degrees.

Peel back fat cover and place garlic cloves on meat, then sprinkle with half of salt/cracked pepper/ garlic salt mixture. Roll fat cover back into place and sprinkle top of fat with remaining salt mixture and herbs.

Place meat on rack in deep roasting pan and roast for 45 minutes. Add to pan chunked vegetables and broths, making sure rack is high enough so liquid doesn't touch meat (you may have to use less broth).

Continue roasting meat until internal temperature reaches 130 degrees. Let rest about half an hour after removing from oven before slicing.

To make gravy, remove roast from pan and place pan on burner. Skim off fat. Bring drippings to a boil, then add cornstarch/water mixture, stirring constantly, until thickened. Adjust seasonings with salt and pepper, strain and keep warm.

Carve meat to whatever thickness you like and serve with gravy and all the trimmings.

CREAMED CHICKEN
WITH HARVARD BEETS
AND GARLIC MASHED POTATOES

SERVES 2 TO 4

Any time you're braising something or making stew, it's important to have whatever meat or poultry you're cooking nearly submerged in water, or stock, or broth. Depending on the size pot you use, you may have to adjust the amount of stock or water I've recommended in my recipes—more for a larger pot, less for a smaller one. Use my recipes as an outline, but use common sense to change them where you need to. Don't ever forget that you're the creator, so you have to use your own judgment accordingly. Learn to adapt whatever you have at home, if you don't have some piece of cooking equipment called for in these pages. You don't have to do things exactly how I do them. I just want to give you a basic idea of how I do something, and then you take it from there.

1   **fryer (2 to 3 lbs.), cut into stewing pieces (make sure you wash out all bone fragments)**
1/4   **lb. butter**
2   **medium onions, diced**
1 or 2 **qts. chicken broth, or enough to cover chicken**
3   **cups heavy cream**
2   **cups mochiko**
Harvard Beets
    (recipe follows)
Garlic Mashed Potatoes
    (see *Sam's Favorite Side Dishes***)**
   salt and pepper to taste
1/2   **cup parsley, chopped**

IN a large Dutch oven, or your favorite covered braising pot, melt butter and brown chicken and onions about 5 to 8 minutes. Stir from time to time on medium heat, until chicken is lightly browned. Add broth to cover and let simmer for 30 minutes.

Skim off fat, add cream, bring to a boil and cook for 2 minutes. Thicken with a paste of mochiko (Japanese sweet rice flour—it really doesn't taste sweet, trust me) mixed with water. Pour the paste slowly into cream sauce and keep stirring and cooking for about 3 minutes, or until it reaches the desired consistency.

Adjust seasoning with salt and pepper to taste, and fold in parsley.

HARVARD BEETS:
2   **cans beets, sliced, or whole baby beets (reserve liquid)**
2   **Tbsp. sugar, or more to taste**
1   **Tbsp. vinegar, or more to taste**
2   **Tbsp. cornstarch mixed with 1-1/2 tbsp. water**
  a dash of white pepper

Bring to a boil the sugar, beet liquid, and vinegar. Gradually add cornstarch mixture, cooking and stirring until you get the consistency you like. You may need to make more cornstarch paste if you want it thicker. Some beets come packed in more liquid than others; you may need to adjust the amount of sugar and vinegar until you get just the right balanced taste of sweet and sour.

Add a dash of white pepper, fold in the beets and heat through. Serve with *Creamed Chicken* and *Garlic Mashed Potatoes.*

YANKEE POT ROAST

SERVES 8 TO 10—OR 6 TO 8 HAWAIIANS

1   **cross rib roast (4 lbs.),**
       or cut of your choice

salt and pepper to taste

1-1/2 Tbsp. garlic, minced

enough flour to dust beef

3   **Tbsp. oil**

2   **medium onions**

2   **medium carrots**

2   **medium potatoes**

4   **stalks celery**

1-1/2 qt. chicken broth, plus 1 qt.
       beef broth, or enough
       to cover meat

3/4   **cup tomato purée**

2   **bay leaves**

1   **sprig rosemary**

enough sweet rice flour and
       water to make thickening
       agent

RUB salt, pepper and garlic on meat and set aside for a few minutes.

Flour meat, then brown on medium heat in the oil until very well browned on all sides, about 10 minutes. Add vegetables, broth, and tomato purée. Bring to a boil. Add bay leaves and rosemary.

Cover and place in a 350-degree oven for 1-1/2 hours, or until fork tender. Other cuts of meat may take longer, up to 3 or even 4 hours, depending on thickness and toughness.

To make gravy, strain out vegetables from drippings. Bring to a boil and thicken with sweet rice flour (it doesn't taste sweet) diluted with water. Cook and stir until you get the consistency you like.

This is one of the easiest "one-pot" dinners you can fix, and with today's slow-cookers it's even easier. All you have to do is set the timer to have it ready when you get home from work. Still, people don't spend enough time in the kitchen to do it right, that's why I want to share my method of doing it.

SUNDAY ROAST CHICKEN WITH STUFFING

SERVES 2 TO 4

1   whole plump fryer
salt and pepper
1   Tbsp. oil
pinch paprika

Rub salt, pepper and oil all over chicken, sprinkle with paprika, then set aside while making stuffing.

STUFFING:

1/2	cup onions, minced
6	slices bacon, chopped
1	stalk celery, minced
1	medium apple, with peel on, chopped
1/2	cup fresh mushrooms, sliced
1/2	stick butter
1/2	cup hot chicken broth or stock
1	Tbsp. parsley, chopped
1	tsp. poultry seasoning
12	oz. dry croutons
1	cup macadamia nuts, coarsely chopped, or nut halves

salt and pepper to taste

IN a large pot, sauté onions, bacon, celery, apples, and mushrooms in butter until onions are translucent. Add chicken broth and bring to a boil. Reduce to simmer. Add parsley and poultry seasoning. Cook for 2 minutes. Add croutons and nuts. Mix well. If bread absorbs all the liquid and seems too dry, you can add a little more broth, or butter. Let cool, then stuff chicken.

Roast at 350 degrees for about 45 minutes to 1 hour, until chicken is done. There's no need to baste. You can make gravy with the pan drippings, if you'd like.

The Legend of the 'Moi Moi Mein'

When we introduced our "Ultimate Stew Omelet," we knew it was designed for serious eaters. Grown men literally passed out when they ate it. Then we came up with the "Moi Moi Mein." We started with a double saimin, then added teriyaki meat, shrimp tempura, fishcake, fresh spinach, a piece of Spam, and Vienna sausage—all in one giant saimin.

Its name, Moi Moi Mein, came about one morning when we served the dish as a breakfast special. I got a phone call that morning from a fellow who explained that he was a supervisor for a construction company and had just flown in to check on a project in Kona.

"Do you see any of my trucks out there?" he asked. I looked outside. "Yeah, I do," I told him. "Can you go and check if the driver is there?" he asked. So I went out and found the braddah passed out, his feet sticking out the window, his head up against his lunch pail—he was out cold. He had just had the Moi Moi Mein.

I woke him up and said, "Eh, brah, your boss is at the airport right now. I told him you were on your way." "Oh, yeah? What time now?" he asked. "Seven-thirty," I told him. He said, "Oh no, I was supposed to pick him up at seven."

After he picked up the boss, they came back to the restaurant together. The boss said, "Eh, Sam, he was telling me about this saimin he just ate." I said, "Oh, you mean the Moi Moi Mein?" "Is that what you guys call it?" he asked. I said, "Yeah, I'm going to name it after him." We all had a good laugh about it, and that is how the Moi Moi Mein got its name.

That's life, you know, it's just life. And that's always been the slogan at my restaurant: Real food for real people.

THE BEST BEEF STEW
SERVES 6

4   lbs. chuck roast, cut up
1/2   cup salad oil
2   cloves garlic, crushed
1   small onion, minced
1/2   cup celery leaves
5   cups beef stock, or broth
2   cups chicken broth
1-1/2 cup tomato paste
3   medium carrots, chunked
4   potatoes, chunked
2   medium onions, chunked
4   stalks celery, chunked
enough flour to dust meat
    (about 1 cup)
salt and pepper to taste
enough mochiko and water
    to thicken

SPRINKLE beef with salt and pepper, then dust with flour. Brown meat with garlic, minced onion, and celery leaves about 10 minutes on medium or low-medium, until well browned. Keep stirring to avoid burning.

Drain oil. Add beef and chicken broth and tomato paste. Bring to a boil, then reduce to simmer. Cover and let cook about 1 hour, or until beef is tender.

Add carrots and potatoes and cook 5 minutes. Add onion chunks and celery and cook 10 minutes more. Adjust seasonings with salt and pepper.

One of my secrets for making a thick, rich stew is that I use mochiko (sweet rice flour) diluted with a little water for thickening. Bring stew to a boil, add sweet rice flour/water mixture a little at a time, simmering and stirring until you get the right consistency. This stew is best the next day, after all the flavors have had a chance to blend.

I think the thing that makes this recipe so good is the simplicity of it, and the fact that very little seasoning is used, letting the natural flavors of the food shine through.

DELUXE MEAT LOAF

SERVES 8 TO 10

1	lb. ground chicken or turkey
1	lb. ground beef
1	lb. ground pork
1	cup day-old bread, diced
3	eggs
1/2	cup onion, chopped
1/2	cup celery, minced
1	cup milk
2	tsp. salt, or to taste
1	Tbsp. shoyu
1/4	tsp. pepper

COMBINE all meat in large mixing bowl. Add bread and mix gently.

In another bowl, beat eggs well. Add onions, celery, milk, and seasonings. Add to meat and stir or knead until well blended, but don't over do it or it will make it tough.

Shape into a loaf and bake in a 350-degree oven for about 1-1/2 hours, or until done.

Lessons from the Road

I've always felt that education is realizing you can never say, "I know it all." We learn every day. I've always felt that traveling, especially trips abroad, is one of the best educational opportunities anyone can have. When I travel and experience other cultures and foreign places, two things are sure to happen. The first thing is I tell myself, "Gee, look at how they do that there; that's really interesting."

For example, the last time I visited Singapore, I got a call from Clyde Min, who's the general manager at the Marina Mandarin Hotel in Singapore. Clyde is originally from Hana, Maui. He called me and said, "Sam, as one local braddah to another, let me take you to a really good restaurant here in Singapore." In a split second I said, "Okay, let's go!"

We went meandering through the back streets of Singapore for what I thought was a very long time, until we finally climbed up to this third floor restaurant. Not knowing any better, I took two steps into the restaurant, and, wow, I thought I was going to get my head chopped off. "Get back out here!" Clyde yelled. I didn't know that you can't just sit down; you have to wait until they seat you. Anyway, I apologized for the mistake and we were eventually seated.

The waitress came over and put a really ugly, banged-up aluminum pot filled with boiling water right on the table. Man, it reminded me of my neighbor's house back in Laie. They kept a lot of dogs and used these banged-up aluminum pots with big black handles as water bowls for the dogs to drink from.

I looked at that pot and wondered if we were supposed to drink it. "No," Clyde said. "You dip all your utensils in there to disinfect the germs." "Then what do we do with it after that?" I asked. "Then we drink 'um up—dat's the soup of the day!" Clyde explained. He was just kidding, but we had a great time laughing and dipping our utensils in the pot. The meal itself, by the way, was outstanding. I especially remember the crab fried rice, which was unbelievable.

That's one of the fascinating things about traveling. I always come home with new experiences, new ideas. Oh, and the second thing that happens whenever I travel is I always come home and tell myself how lucky I am to live in Hawai'i, and to never take that good fortune for granted.

PAPA'S LUAU FEAST

Claire Wai Sun Choy

In many ways, my sister, Claire Wai Sun Choy, has been a key person behind much that I've accomplished in the restaurant business.

She was actually trained to be a schoolteacher, but couldn't get a teaching job when she moved to Waikoloa in 1973. When she heard that one of the hotels was looking for a cook, she went in and applied. She told the guy, "I'm not trained as a cook, but if you're willing to teach me, I'm willing to learn. If I can't cut it, let me go." She'd call me up from time to time for advice, but she basically took to it "like a duck to water."

Later, Wai Sun returned to Oahu to study food service at KCC and even had the opportunity to travel with the KCC program to Europe. After she graduated from that program, she was hired as one of the original chefs at the John Dominis restaurant. From there she moved over to the Lokelani Room at the Maui Marriott. Just six months after they opened, she told the food and beverage manager, "I don't think tourists want to come all the way to Hawai'i and be given a choice between salmon and veal marsala—just because we put a pineapple and an orchid on the plate doesn't make it Hawaiian." Convinced by her logic, the food and beverage manager authorized her to change the menus, the whole concept of the restaurant.

Wai Sun was working at the Marriott when I came up with the idea of opening Sam's Place in Laie in 1981. I was working at the Turtle Bay Hilton at the time, and I convinced her to leave her job and came home to run the family restaurant.

Later, when I was the executive chef at the Kona Hilton, the hotel was hit by a big strike, around 1989 or 1990. The whole crew walked out, including my sous chef. I called Wai Sun up and asked her to help me. Fortunately, she flew over and helped me out at the Kona Hilton for a couple of weeks. One thing led to another, and we later opened the diner at the bowling alley, as well as the restaurant in 1991.

Today, she runs the bowling alley and takes care of a lot of the operational details of both restaurants. Along with my wife, Carol, and sister Wai Lin Choy, it's still a family affair.

TRADITIONAL LOMI LOMI SALMON

SERVES 24

4	cups salted salmon, diced
12	tomatoes, diced
4	small red onions, diced
1	cup green onion, thinly sliced
1-2	Hawaiian chili peppers, or
1/4	tsp. red pepper flakes (optional)

COMBINE all ingredients and mix well. Serve well chilled. (Salted salmon comes with various degrees of saltiness, so it's a good idea to taste it before making this dish. If it's too salty, you need to soak it overnight in enough water to cover, and then rinse it twice before using.)

Here in Hawai'i the luau is the traditional way of celebrating a special occasion. On any given weekend, you will find luau going on all over. They are held for birthdays, anniversaries, weddings, grand openings of new businesses, blessings of boats, the opening or closing of a special event, and for any other reason somebody feels like celebrating. And we're not talking pupu or crackers and cheese—this is heavy eating, true feasting. It's a tradition in Hawai'i to hold a baby luau on your child's first birthday, as a way of giving thanks that your baby made it through the first year, because in the old days lots of babies didn't make it to their first birthday. Anywhere from 50 to 5,000 people will show up for one of these baby luau, and it's real festive, with Hawaiian entertainment and endless food, and it can go on for two or three days. I learned to cook as a kid helping my dad cater luau in Laie. I've included only a few of my favorite luau recipes here; a big luau will have many additional dishes.

NO-IMU KALUA PIG

SERVES 24

The traditional way to cook a whole pig Hawaiian-style is in an underground oven, or imu. It's a lot of work and it takes all day, but, man, does it taste good. Lots of people still do it this way for parties and special events, but you can also do it in your oven with a lot less hassle, and it tastes almost as good.

8	lbs. pork butt
4	Tbsp. liquid smoke
4	Tbsp. Hawaiian salt
8-12	large ti leaves, ribs removed

PREHEAT oven to 350 degrees. After scoring pork on all sides with quarter-inch deep slits about an inch apart, rub with salt, then liquid smoke. Wrap the pork completely in ti leaves, tie with string, and wrap in foil.

Place meat in a shallow roasting pan with 2 cups of water and roast for 4 hours.

Dissolve 1 tablespoon Hawaiian salt in 2 cups boiling water and add a few drops of liquid smoke. Shred the cooked pork and let stand in this solution for a few minutes before serving.

MY MOM'S SQUID LUAU

SERVES 12

2	lbs. calamari
3	lbs. luau leaves
1	Tbsp. Hawaiian salt
1/2	tsp. baking soda
6	Tbsp. butter
2	medium onions, diced
3	cups coconut milk
1-1/2	tsp. salt
1	Tbsp. sugar

CLEAN calamari and slice in rings, then set aside.

Wash luau leaves, remove stems and thick veins. In a pot, boil 3 cups of water with the Hawaiian salt and baking soda. Add the leaves to the boiling water and reduce heat. Simmer, partially covered, for 1 hour. Drain, and squeeze out liquid.

Sauté onions and calamari in butter until the onions are translucent. Add the coconut milk, cooked luau leaves, salt, and sugar. Simmer for 30 minutes.

CAN'T GET ENOUGH OTARU POKE

SERVES 24

"Otaru" is the Japanese word for a large aku, a member of the tuna family, also known as bonito. If you can't get otaru, a small aku, or some ahi will do just as well.

2	lbs. otaru, or raw fish of your choice, cubed
2	tomatoes, chopped
2	cups limu, chopped
1	cup onion, chopped
4	Tbsp. shoyu
2	tsp. sesame oil
1	Hawaiian chili pepper, minced, or 1 tsp. red pepper flakes

Mix everything together well and chill until ice-cold.

DA KINE POKE SUPREME

SERVES 24

2	cups raw ahi, cubed
1	cup opihi, or poached scallops, or cooked mussels
6	whole crabs, cleaned and lightly salted, quartered
2	lbs. cooked octopus, thinly sliced
1/2	cup ogo, chopped
1	cup limu wawae'iole (rat's feet seaweed or miru), coarsely chopped
2	tomatoes, chopped
2	cups cucumbers, chopped
1	cup onion, chopped
6	Tbsp. shoyu
2	tsp. sesame oil
1	tsp. red pepper flakes, or 1 Hawaiian chili pepper

Mix ingredients well and chill until ice-cold.

POI

SERVES 12

3   lbs. taro corms, peeled and boiled and diced into 1-in. cubes

3   cups water

MASH boiled taro in a wooden bowl with a wooden potato masher until you've turned it into a thick paste. Little by little, work in the water with your hands, then force the poi through several thicknesses of cheesecloth to remove lumps and fiber.

Serve it fresh, or let it ferment for that distinctive sour taste by allowing it to stand for 2 or 3 days in a cool place.

You must have poi with your luau whether you like it or not. It just isn't a luau without it. Poi has been a Hawaiian staple for thousands of years. It is very nutritious and good for you, and if you sample it often enough, you will eventually acquire a taste for it—maybe. If you're not used to it, it's best to eat it when it's very fresh, although some people like it better after it has sat around for a few days and become sour. I don't recommend making it yourself, as it's a lot of work and very time-consuming, and you can't beat the commercial variety found in grocery stores. But just in case you're feeling ambitious, I've included this simple recipe.

CHICKEN LONG RICE

SERVES 12

2	lbs. chicken, skin and bones removed, cubed
4	cups chicken broth
2-in.	finger of fresh ginger, crushed
1	medium onion, minced
2	cups celery, sliced thin
2	carrots, julienned
20	shiitake mushrooms
4	oz. long rice
6	green onions, cut in 1-in. lengths

SOAK long rice in warm water for 1 hour. Soak mushrooms in warm water for 20 minutes, drain, then remove stems and slice caps.

Pour chicken broth into a large pot, add chicken and ginger, and simmer for 5 minutes. Add onion, celery, carrots, and mushrooms, and simmer for another 4 to 5 minutes.

Drain long rice and cut into 3-inch lengths. Add green onions and long rice to pot and cook 5 minutes, or until long rice becomes translucent.

SWEET POTATO PALAU

SERVES 12

6   **medium yams or sweet potatoes**

1/2 **cup sugar, more or less, to taste**

1   **cup fresh or canned coconut milk**

BOIL whole sweet potatoes or yams for 1 hour, or until tender. Cool until easily handled, then peel off skin and mash. Fold in sugar and coconut milk and whip until fluffy. Some sweet potatoes and yams are sweeter than others, so you need to add the sugar gradually and keep tasting as you go, until you get the desired sweetness. Chill until very cold. Yummy.

Sweet potatoes and coconuts, along with taro, were main staples of the ancient Hawaiian diet. Wild sugar cane was used to sweeten food.

PINEAPPLE HAUPIA

SERVES 12

6   cups canned or fresh
     coconut milk

1   cup cornstarch

1   cup sugar

1/2   tsp. salt

1   cup crushed pineapple

DRAIN pineapple, squeeze out excess liquid and set aside.

Combine coconut milk, cornstarch, sugar, and salt. Stir until cornstarch is dissolved. Cook on medium heat, stirring constantly, until it reaches the boiling point, then reduce to low. When it begins to thicken, add the pineapple and mix well.

Pour into individual dessert bowls, or sorbet glasses, and serve either warm or cold, topped with whipped cream. To serve cold, chill for at least 1 hour.

This simple but delicious pudding goes way back, to the days when the Hawaiians had only fruit, coconuts, and wild sugar cane for sweets. I've given it a little twist by adding crushed pineapple.

SIDE DISHES

GARLIC MASHED POTATOES _____ 183

BOK CHOY BROCCOLI _____ 183

QUICK SNOW PEAS _____ 184

GINGER CARROTS _____ 184

STUFFED PEPPERS, ORIENTAL STYLE _____ 185

CHINESE CABBAGE TOSS _____ 185

BLACK GOMA ASPARAGUS _____ 187

BACON LETTUCE LEAVES _____ 188

ISLAND JI _____ 189

MACADAMIA NUT EGGPLANT _____ 190

Side dishes are very important. They give you a bonus. People remember a great meal not only for the entrée, but just as much for the sides. They are always a highlight for me. Eating in Hawai'i is so interesting because we have so many styles of side dishes originating in so many diverse cultures, from Southeast-Asian pickled, steamed, and stir-fried vegetables, to Portuguese sweet bread, Japanese tempura, Korean kimchee, Hawaiian poke, and good ol' American baked beans and cole slaw.

GARLIC MASHED POTATOES

SERVES 4

2-1/4 lbs. potatoes
4 whole cloves garlic
1/2 lb. butter
3 oz. cream
white pepper and salt, to taste

PEEL and cut the potatoes into 1-inch cubes.

In a pot, cover the potatoes with cold water, add garlic and bring to a boil. Cook for 8 to 10 minutes, or until done. Drain. Purée in a food processor, or whip with an electric mixer. Add the butter and cream. Season with salt and white pepper. Serve immediately.

BOK CHOY BROCCOLI

SERVES 6

2 Tbsp. cooking oil
1 medium onion, thinly sliced
1 Tbsp. fresh ginger root, grated or minced
2 cloves garlic, crushed
1/2 tsp. salt
3 cups fresh broccoli florets, sliced
1 lb. bok choy, coarsely chopped
2 Tbsp. lemon juice
1-1/2 tsp. sugar
1 Tbsp. shoyu

HEAT oil in wok or skillet on medium-high until it's almost smoking. Add onion, ginger, garlic, and salt. Stir-fry for 2 minutes. Add broccoli and bok choy and stir-fry for 1 minute. Add lemon juice, sugar, and shoyu and stir-fry for 3 minutes, or until crisp-tender.

QUICK SNOW PEAS

SERVES 4

1/4   cup oil

4   cups fresh snow peas

2   cloves garlic, minced

1-1/2 tsp. shoyu

1-1/2 tsp. oyster sauce

2   Tbsp. chicken broth

HEAT oil in wok or skillet on medium-high. Stir-fry snow peas for 1 minute. Reduce heat and continue to stir-fry for another minute. Drain off excess oil. Sprinkle snow peas with garlic, shoyu, oyster sauce, and broth. Simmer gently for 1-1/2 minutes.

GINGER CARROTS

SERVES 6

6   large carrots

3   Tbsp. butter

1/4   tsp. salt

1   Tbsp. fresh ginger, grated

2   Tbsp. brown sugar

CUT carrots into bite-sized pieces. Steam until tender. Add remaining ingredients and stir for a minute or two, until carrots are glazed.

STUFFED PEPPERS, ORIENTAL STYLE

SERVES 4

8	red or yellow bell peppers
2	Tbsp. cooking oil
3	green onions, chopped
1	tsp. garlic, minced
1	small finger fresh ginger, minced
2	Tbsp. Chinese parsley, chopped
2	oz. fresh bean sprouts
2	Tbsp., or more, shoyu
1	can water chestnuts, chopped
3	cups cooked rice
1	cup cooked vegetables of your choice, diced
1	egg, beaten
	salt and pepper to taste

COOK peppers in boiling water for 5 minutes. Remove and cool. Slice off tops, scoop out seeds and membranes. Set aside.

Heat oil and stir-fry onion, garlic, ginger, and parsley until crisp-tender. Add sprouts and shoyu and cook just until sprouts wilt. Remove from heat.

Add water chestnuts, rice, cooked vegetables, egg, and salt and pepper. Toss together until well mixed. Add more shoyu, if desired. Spoon into pepper cases.

Place in a baking dish containing 1/2 inch hot water. Cover with foil and bake at 350 degrees for 30 minutes. Uncover and bake another 15 to 20 minutes, or until peppers are tender.

CHINESE CABBAGE TOSS

SERVES 4 TO 6

This light salad is quick and easy to make and goes well with heavy meat dishes.

2	lb. Chinese white cabbage
1	tsp. salt
2	tsp. sugar
2	Tbsp. shoyu
1	Tbsp. salad oil
1/2	Tbsp. sesame oil

CUT cabbage into strips 3 inches long by 1/2 inch wide and blanch in boiling water for 2 minutes, then drain. Dry well and place in large bowl. Add salt, sugar, shoyu and oils. Toss well and serve.

BLACK GOMA ASPARAGUS

1   lb. asparagus
3   slices fresh ginger
1/4   cup chicken broth
1   Tbsp. shoyu
1/2   tsp. sugar
2   Tbsp. oil
1/2   tsp. salt
1   tsp. black goma

WASH asparagus, break off tough ends and discard. Cut stalks diagonally in 1-1/2-inch sections. If the asparagus is young and tender, blanch stalks (but not tips) by immersing quickly in boiling water and rinsing immediately under cold water. Mature asparagus should be parboiled in salted water for a minute or 2, removed as soon as it begins to turn bright green, and rinsed immediately in cold water and drained. Do not blanch or parboil the tips.

Mince or crush the ginger. Combine broth, shoyu, and sugar. Heat the oil on medium-high and, when it's almost smoking, add the salt and ginger and stir-fry a few times. Add asparagus and stir-fry until heated through. You may have to adjust the heat to prevent scorching.

Add broth mixture and heat quickly. Simmer, covered, over medium heat for 2 to 3 minutes. Sprinkle with black goma and serve.

BACON LETTUCE LEAVES

SERVES 4

8   slices bacon

1/4   cup vinegar

2   Tbsp. sugar

2   Tbsp. water

salt and pepper to taste

2   heads leaf lettuce
      (try Harvey's Sun Bear), torn
      into bite-sized pieces

1/2 cup macadamia nuts, chopped

FRY bacon until crisp, remove from pan, drain, chop and set aside.

Pour vinegar into bacon fat in pan. Add sugar and water and bring to a boil. Salt and pepper to taste.

Pour hot mixture over lettuce. Add nuts, toss, and garnish with chopped bacon.

ISLAND JI

SERVES 8 TO 10

In small portions this traditional Buddhist monk food makes an interesting side dish, or you can make an entire meal of it.

1-2   cups vegetable broth,
       or chicken broth

3   Tbsp. shoyu

1   tsp. sherry

4   Tbsp. oil

1/8   lb. rice noodles, soaked,
       cut in 3-in. lengths

1/2   cup dried black mushrooms,
       soaked, cut in half

3   sticks dried bean curd,
       broken in 2-in. lengths
       and soaked

1/2   cup onion, thinly sliced

1/2   cup bean sprouts, blanched

1/2   cup cauliflower,
       broken into small florets

1/2   cup Chinese cabbage,
       cut in 2-in. sections

1/2   cup snow peas, stemmed

1   cup zucchini,
       cut in 2-in. slices

1   cup canned bamboo shoots,
       sliced into thin shreds

1/2   cup raw peanuts,
       whole or chopped

1   Tbsp. cornstarch

pinch of sugar

3   Tbsp. water

1   tsp. shoyu

few drops of sesame oil

COMBINE broth, 3 tablespoons shoyu, and sherry. Set aside. Heat oil and stir-fry next 11 ingredients 3 to 5 minutes. If you don't have a large wok or skillet, cook three or four ingredients at a time. Mix everything together before adding cornstarch paste. Add broth/*shoyu*/sherry mixture and heat quickly. Simmer, covered, 10 to 15 minutes, until vegetables are tender.

Blend cornstarch, sugar, cold water, and 1 teaspoon shoyu to make a paste. Add to vegetables, stirring until thickened. Sprinkle with a few drops of sesame oil, stir in, and serve.

This vegetarian dish is known by Buddhists as the Feast of Arahats, or Food for the Saints, and is included in nearly every Chinese New Year feast. There are many variations of it—feel free to experiment, using your favorite ingredients. It will keep about a week in the refrigerator and can be reheated several times without losing its flavor.

MACADAMIA NUT EGGPLANT

SERVES 6

3   eggplants

1/3   cup oil

1   onion, minced

1   clove garlic, minced

salt and pepper to taste

1   tomato, peeled and chopped

1   tsp. worcestershire sauce

2   eggs, lightly beaten

1   cup macadamia nuts, chopped

1/2   cup soft buttered bread crumbs

CUT the eggplants in half lengthwise and scoop out the insides, leaving about a quarter-inch shell. Mince the pulp.

Heat oil in a skillet and cook onion and garlic until tender. Add minced eggplant and cook slowly until lightly browned and almost tender. Season with salt and pepper. Add the tomato and worcestershire and simmer 3 minutes. Stir in the eggs and nuts. Mix well.

Stuff the eggplant shells and top with bread crumbs. Set in a shallow greased roasting pan. Bake at 375 degrees for 25 minutes, or until eggplant shells are tender.

'Mele Mele' Mango Memories

I really don't know if it's my place to say so or not, but I sometimes want to tell our children, "Hey, look, you guys are missing out. Maybe you don't need to have fancy cars, a certain kind of hairdo, or a lot money in your pocket to find the identity you're searching for. Maybe you need to appreciate what we have here in Hawaii. Maybe you need to give the islands a chance."

As kids, I remember we'd have fun just walking along the beach early in the morning looking for glass balls, or walking in the mountains—smelling the beautiful rain coming off of the trees and being sheltered by the leaves. We knew where ice cold spring water came gushing out of the mountain. I thought that was the highest high you could get. Sometimes, the simple things in life are the most amazing.

The tropical seasons offered us variety. Mango season was a big thing for us. Everybody would go out to look for mangos up in the hills in back of Laie. We had our own names for these common mango groves, like Kakiyama and CPC. We'd send out search parties that would come back with their reports. "Ready?" "No, not ready. Still green yet." When the mangos ripened, we'd throw rocks at the branches to knock the fruit down. We were always making up our own slang, and, for some reason, "mele-mele" came to mean a really-really ripe mango. If we spotted a mele-mele mango, about ten guys would be throwing rocks trying to get the ripe fruit.

I was too short and chunky to climb the trees, but some of the kids would climb up to the top of the branches and shout down to the kids below, "Ready?" "Ready!" we'd shout back. Then they'd start swinging and shaking the branches. "Whoo-hahh . . ." And all these mangos would rain down on us. We'd pick up the mangos and sit by the side of the canefield road, peeling and eating them.

When plum season came around, everybody would carry their mayonnaise bottles filled with a homemade sauce of a little shoyu, sugar, and vinegar. We'd take our bottles up to the mountain, pick the little purple plums, and put them in the bottle. Then, we'd mash 'em with a stick, and let them sit overnight. The next day, man, your lips would just pucker up. It tasted so good.

There was guava season and mountain apple season, and sometimes we'd go up to the mountains to pick ginger blossoms—tons of ginger to bring home and make leis. It was unbelievable, going through all those seasons.

Parts of Laie and Kahuku were also used as military training areas. We kids found out that the soldiers didn't take back all of their C rations. They would bury the unopened C ration cans in the ground. We'd go up and rake the mountains for their cases of C rations and haul them all back home and get into some hot trading sessions. "I'll trade you scramble eggs and ham for one of your chocolates." "Okay, and I'll give you two powdered milk for one peanut butter."

Those are just some of the wonderful memories I have of the way we grew up. I realize we can't turn back the hands of time, and sometimes it doesn't help to dwell on things we can't control. However, there are still many wonderful aspects of Hawaii that we tend to neglect. It's a matter of priorities, I guess. But when we don't give these islands a chance, I think we really lose out.

DESSERTS

My wife, Carol, is the real dessert expert in our family. She makes the best turnovers and the best double-crusted pies in the world. I enjoy watching her bake and helping her, but she always kicks me out of the kitchen 'cuz she says baking is not like cooking—you can't just throw in a little of this and a little of that. She says it's more of a science; it has to be exact, you can't be innovative as I like to be; you have to stick to the recipe. She's taught me a lot about baking, but she's still better at it than I am. None of the following dessert recipes are original with me. Just as I love to share my favorite recipes, so do my friends and neighbors, and these are a few that get passed around a lot.

MACADAMIA NUT BANANA CAKE

1-3/4 cups butter

2 cups sugar

4 cups flour

1 Tbsp. baking powder

6 eggs

1 lb. raw macadamia nuts, coarsely chopped

1 lb. firm apple bananas, chopped

2 Tbsp. vanilla extract

PREHEAT oven to 250 degrees. Cream butter and sugar. Measure sifted flour, then sift with baking powder. Add eggs and flour, alternately, to creamed butter/sugar. Add nuts, chopped bananas, and vanilla.

Pour into a large, well-greased tube pan (the kind you make angel food cake in). Before baking, place a pan of water on the oven rack below.

Bake at 250 for 2 to 3 hours. Test for doneness with a toothpick.

PAPAYA PASSION FRUIT CAKE

1/2   cup butter
1   cup sugar
2   eggs, beaten
1   cup papaya, mashed
2   cups flour
1/2   tsp. cinnamon
1/2   tsp. salt
3/4   tsp. baking powder
1   tsp. baking soda
1/2   tsp. allspice
1/2   tsp. cloves
1/2   cup macadamia nuts, chopped

PREHEAT oven to 350 degrees.

Cream butter, add sugar gradually, then add beaten eggs and mashed papaya. Sift flour before measuring. Mix and sift dry ingredients and add to creamed butter mixture.

Pour into greased and floured rectangular cake pan and bake for 25 minutes, or until toothpick comes out clean, and ice with the following.

PASSION FRUIT ICING:

3   Tbsp. butter
2-1/4   cups confectioners sugar
3   Tbsp. fresh passion fruit juice
1/3   cup macadamia nuts, coarsely chopped
1/3   cup coconut, shredded

Cream butter. Add sugar gradually and cream until fluffy. Add passion fruit juice, beating until the icing is smooth and stiff enough to spread on the cake.

Sprinkle chopped nuts and coconut over the icing. If passion fruit isn't in season, you can use frozen passion fruit juice, but because it's sweetened, your icing will be sweeter.

MANGO BREAD

1/2 cup butter
1 cup sugar
2 eggs
2 cups flour
1 tsp. baking soda
2 cups mango, finely minced
1/4 cup macadamia nuts,
    or your favorite nutmeats,
    chopped

PREHEAT oven to 350 degrees. Cream butter and sugar. Add eggs one at a time and beat well. Sift dry ingredients and add alternately with mango pulp. Add nuts.

Pour into a greased and floured loaf pan. Bake at 350 degrees for about an hour. Test for doneness with a toothpick. (If you can't get mango, substitute mashed papaya or other fruit.)

LILIKOI CHIFFON CREAM PIE

1 Tbsp. unflavored gelatin
1/4 cup cold water
4 eggs, separated
1 cup sugar
1/2 tsp. salt
1/2 cup fresh lilikoi juice
1 tsp. lemon rind, grated
1 baked pie shell
1/2 cup cream, whipped
enough toasted shredded
    coconut to sprinkle on top

YOU have to use fresh yellow lilikoi juice for this recipe.

Soften the gelatin in the water. Beat the egg yolks until thick and add 1/2 cup of the sugar, the salt, and the lilikoi juice. Mix well.

Cook, stirring, over low heat until thickened, about 10 minutes. Add gelatin mixture and stir until the gelatin is dissolved. Remove from heat. Add lemon rind and cool until slightly congealed. Beat egg whites with remaining 1/2 cup of sugar, until stiff, and fold in.

Pour into a cooled, baked pie shell and chill until firm. Top with whipped cream and sprinkles of toasted coconut.

MACADAMIA NUT PIE

3   eggs
2/3 cup sugar
1   cup light corn syrup
1-1/2 to 2 cups chopped
     macadamia nuts
2   Tbsp. melted butter
1   tsp. vanilla
1   unbaked 9-in. pie shell

BEAT eggs with sugar and corn syrup. Stir in the nuts. Add butter and vanilla and blend well.

Pour mixture into pie shell. Bake at 325 degrees for 50 minutes, or until the crust is golden and the center is somewhat set—test by shaking gently. Let cool and chill.

EASY BANANA PIE

1 8-oz. pkg. cream cheese, softened
1 cup dairy sour cream
3 Tbsp. sugar
3 cups bananas, sliced, dipped in lime or lemon juice
Graham Cracker Crust
   whipped cream

BLEND cream cheese and sour cream. Add sugar and mix well. Add bananas.

Pour into graham cracker crust. Freeze firm. Remove from freezer 5 minutes before serving. Top with whipped cream.

GRAHAM CRACKER CRUST:

Combine 1 cup fine graham cracker crumbs, 2 tablespoons sugar and 3 tablespoons melted butter or margarine. Press firmly into unbuttered 9-inch pie plate by pressing down with another pie plate. Chill until firm, about 45 minutes.

PINEAPPLE COCONUT YUM YUM

BOTTOM CRUST:
1 cup butter
2/3 cup sugar
1/2 tsp. vanilla
1-1/2 cup flour
1 cup macadamia nuts, chopped

FILLING:
1 cup sugar
1 Tbsp. cornstarch
1 can (No. 2) crushed pineapple with juice
1/2 cup coconut, shredded

TOPPING:
1/2 cup sugar
1/2 cup butter
1/4 cup flour
2 cups oatmeal

TO make bottom crust, cream butter and sugar. Add vanilla, flour and nuts. Press into the bottom of a 9-inch by 13-inch pan and bake for 10 minutes in a preheated 350-degree oven.

To make the filling, combine sugar and cornstarch in a small saucepan. Add the crushed pineapple and pineapple juice. Cook over medium heat until thickened. Add the coconut and pour over crust.

For the topping, cream the sugar and butter. Mix in the flour. Add oatmeal and blend well. Cut dough into the size of peas and sprinkle evenly over the filling. Pat down firmly. Bake at 350 degrees for about 35 minutes, or until lightly browned.

PAPAYA SORBET
SERVES 6

2-1/2 cups papaya, sliced
1   cup sugar
1   Tbsp. fresh lemon
      or lime juice
2   Tbsp. gelatin
1/2 cup cold water
2   cups cream

MASH papaya, add sugar, and cook for 5 minutes in a saucepan. Remove from heat and put through a colander to strain. Add lemon or lime juice. Soak gelatin in cold water, add papaya mixture and stir well. Cool and chill.

Add 1-1/2 cups cream and freeze until slushy. Whip 1/2 cup cream until very light and stir into mixture. Freeze again.

GINGER PINEAPPLE SORBET

SERVES 6

1	cup sugar
1/2	cup pineapple juice
1	Tbsp. fresh lemon
	or orange juice
1	Tbsp. fresh ginger, grated
1	pt. cream

MIX ingredients. Place in freezer until partially frozen, then put in a bowl and mix well with a wooden spoon, or beat slowly. Return to freezer until frozen.

GUAVA MOUSSE

SERVES 6

1/2	cup guava pulp, strained
1/2	cup sugar
1	cup heavy cream, whipped

COMBINE guava pulp and sugar. Fold into whipped cream. Pour into freezing tray and freeze until firm.

Glossary

ahi - yellowfin tuna with reddish-pink flesh

aku - bonito, skipjack tuna with deep red firm flesh

al dente - firm to the bite, chewy

au - swordfish, marlin

bok choy (bok choi) - oriental cabbage (substitute white cabbage)

bean threads - long rice, cellophane noodles

bonito flakes - oriental shaved dried fish

butterfish - black cod with a strong flavor (substitute bluefish)

Chinese parsley - cilantro, a strong-flavored herb

coho salmon - a comparatively small salmon native to the N. Pacific Ocean

cumin - seasoning used in curry and chili powders; from the parsley family

daikon - radish-flavored root (substitute turnips)

dashi - Japanese fish stock

dashikonbu - Japanese fish stock with seaweed

devein - to remove the vein-like intestine from shrimp or other shellfish

Five star spice - oriental licorice flavoring

flank steak - a cut of beef between the ribs and the hip

goma - sesame seed

Hawaiian salt - sea salt

hibachi - a small, charcoal-burning grill

Hoisin sauce - sauce of fermented soy beans, garlic, rice, salt and sugar

imu - underground oven

julienned - cut into thin strips

lau lau - packages of ti leaves or banana leaves containing pork, beef, salted fish, or taro tops, baked in the ground oven, steamed or broiled

lilikoi - tangy, plum-sized passion fruit (substitute orange juice)

limu - edible sea salad

lomilomi - to rub, press, squeeze, knead, massage

luau (leaves) - young taro tops (substitute spinach)

lychee - small, sweet white fruit in a hard shell (available canned)

mahimahi - dolphin fish with firm, light pink flesh

mirin - Japanese sweet rice wine (substitute one teaspoon sugar for one tablespoon mirin)

mochiko - Japanese sweet rice flour

napa - Chinese cabbage

nasturtiums - flowers

nori - thin sheets of dried seaweed

ogo - seaweed

onaga - red snapper with pink flesh

ong choy - swamp cabbage

ono - wahoo with white flaky texture; also, delicious, tasty, savory

opah - a very large, brightly colored, silvery, marine bony fish

opakapaka - pink snapper with firm light pink flesh

opal basil - purple basil

opihi - limpet

otaru - large tuna

panko - crispy flour meal (substitute coarse white bread crumbs)

phyllo (dough) - dough in very thin sheets which becomes very flaky when baked

poha - cape gooseberries

poke - to slice, cut crosswise into pieces, as fish or wood

Portuguese sausage - hot pork sausage (substitute spicy Italian sausage)

pupu - appetizer

sake - Japanese rice wine

sashimi - thin slices of fresh raw fish

shiitake - dried mushrooms with a meaty flavor

shoyu - brown liquid of soy beans, barley and salt (also called soy sauce)

soba - Japanese angel hair pasta

spring mix greens - assortment of five or more delicate salad leaves

spring roll skin - rice paper wrapper (lumpia)

steamer basket - bamboo steamer basket

taro - starchy edible root

ti (leaf) - a Polynesian and Australian woody plant of the agave family

tutu - grandmother

uku - gray snapper with firm pink flesh

wasabi - hot green Japanese horseradish

weke ula - goat fish

won bok - (Chinese cabbage; also napa)

won ton wrapper - rice paper

Index

Index

SAM CHOY

Sam Choy was born and raised in the town of Laie, on the North Shore of the island of Oahu. The second of four children born to Hang Sam and Clairemoana Choy, Sam developed his keen taste for island food from his parents, who operated a small general store in Laie.

Starting in the early 1950s, and continuing on through the '60s, Sam's father catered the food for the Mormon Church luau and hukilau, held in Laie every Saturday. Still in elementary school, Sam helped his father prepare the food for as many as 800 people at a time.

After graduating from Kahuku High School in 1970, Sam attended Columbia Basin Junior College in Washington state on a football scholarship. When injuries ended his football playing dreams, Sam returned to Hawai'i. After months of indecision and half-hearted attempts at resuming his schooling, Sam's mother urged him to enroll in Kapiolani Community College's highly regarded food service program. Although he enjoyed cooking, Sam had never thought to pursue it as a career. "I always thought you gotta cook if you wanna eat. I never thought of it as being a profession that would support you and your family."

His experience at cooking school was a complete revelation. "It was just like a switch came on in my head," he explains. "I got so excited, I began thinking constantly about ways I could take food to higher and higher levels."

Sam's first job was at the then Hyatt Kuilima Resort on Oahu's North Shore, now the Turtle Bay Hilton & Country Club. Starting as a cook's helper, Sam worked his way up to dinner cook, sous chef, and executive sous chef. While at the Hilton, Sam had the opportunity to work at New York's famed Waldorf Astoria, an experience that gave him his first look at the world of international cuisine. Before long, Sam was garnering awards himself, including a gold medal at the American Culinary Federation's Culinary Competition of the Pacific.

In 1981, Sam and his family opened a small restaurant called Sam's Place next to his father's store in Laie. It was there that the family's natural penchant for turning out great local-style meals was introduced to the public. Sam's next big break came in 1986, when he was named executive chef of the Kona Hilton Beach & Tennis Resort on the Big Island of Hawai'i. For Sam, this was the fulfillment of a lifelong dream. He resettled in Kona, where he now lives with his wife, Carol, and sons Sam, Jr. and Christopher. During his five years at the helm of the Kona Hilton's dining room, Sam's lavish Sunday brunches and imaginative menu items helped put the hotel on the culinary map, and Sam's fame spread throughout the islands—and beyond.

In 1991, Sam, in partnership with his sister Wai Sun, opened Sam Choy's Diner in a bowling alley in Kailua-Kona and Sam Choy's Restaurant in the Koloko Light Industrial Park. A third restaurant, Sam Choy's Diamond Head, recently opened on Oahu, on Kapahulu Avenue. All of Sam Choy's eateries are renowned for their delicious food—classic, Island-style flavors; generous portions; good service; comfortable settings; and reasonable prices—a winning formula in anyone's book.

ARNOLD T. HIURA

Arnold T. Hiura is the former editor of *The Hawaii Herald.* For the past two-and-a-half years, he and partner Glen Grant have collaborated as writers, editors and creative consultants on a wide variety of projects. Grant & Hiura assisted in the production of such recent publications as: *Manoa: The Story of a Valley, Boyhood to War: The History of the 442nd Regimental Combat Team, A History of Service: The Central Pacific Bank Story, Adios to Tears, Getting the Edge: Hawaii Football* and the runaway bestseller *Obake: Ghost Stories of Hawaii.*

EVELYN COOK

Evelyn Cook is a journalist who has worked for the past 20 years as a daily newspaper reporter, magazine editor, columnist, and ghost writer. She lives on Kauai with her husband, Chris, and two sons, Christian, 10, and David, 6.

MICHAEL A. HORTON

Michael A. Horton has designed numerous books, including *Hawaii: The Royal Legacy* and *'Onipa'a: Five Days in the History of the Hawaiian Nation,* both of which received awards of excellence for design. His studio, Michael Horton Design, is located in Aiea, O'ahu, and specializes in a wide variety of graphic design capabilities, including; corporate identity, sign systems, collateral and packaging.

DOUGLAS PEEBLES

Douglas Peebles has been capturing the beauty of Hawai'i on film for a number of years. He has published many of these images in his book series, *Skies of Paradise Hawai'i* and *Pua Nani.* His photography appears regularly in magazines, annual reports and other publications. Douglas' studio is located in Kailua, O'ahu.

FAITH OGAWA

Food Stylist Faith Ogawa gained her love for cooking from her grandmother, a Waipahu farmer originally from Okinawa. A graduate of Leeward Community College in the Culinary Arts, Faith has spent the last 20 years in the food industry in Hawai'i and abroad as a professional chef, an instructor at Kapiolani Community College and most recently, as a restaurant manager at the Mauna Lani Bay Hotel and Bungalows. In each capacity Faith always incorporates Hawai'i's healthful foods, unique and spirit of Aloha in all her work. She lives in Waimea, Hawai'i with her son Kahlil, 10.

Kau Kau!

COOKING NOTES

COOKING NOTES